ECOcentric Topics

PIONEERING THEMES
FOR ECO-ART

LINDA WEINTRAUB

with SKIP SCHUCKMANN

AVANT-GUARDIANS
TEXTLETS ON ART AND ECOLOGY

ARTNOW PUBLICATIONS
RHINEBECK, NEW YORK

ECOcentric Topics
Pioneering Themes for Eco-Art

Avant-Guardians: Textlets on Art and Ecology

Linda Weintraub with Skip Schuckmann

Publication 2006 Artnow Publications
Texts Copyright Linda Weintraub
28 Olsen Road, Rhinebeck, NY 12572
Tel. 845 758-9289. artnow@juno.com
Collaborator: Skip Schuckmann
Editor: Dan Franck
Primary typefaces: Optima, Zapfino
Print-to-order
Published by Artnow Publications
28 Olsen Road
Rhinebeck, NY 12572
ISBN 0-9777421-4-8
SAN: 859-1181
First Edition
Library of Congress Cataloguing-in-Publication Data

Contents

Preface

Sandwiched between a 60-pound dog and a 20-pound baby in the back of an eight-seater van for a four-hour drive that was likely to feel like a month, I decided to occupy myself by seeking evidence of all 10 themes I had just chosen for a textlet on art and ecology. Esoteric speculation and abstract theorizing were not the goals. These themes had been chosen for their timeliness, relevance, and edifying potential. Thus, as trees whizzed by along the highway and the rhythmic murmur of sleeping bodies came from my left and my right, I began my accountings by asking, "What is the source of the impulse to leave 'here' and arrive 'there'?" The answer came quite quickly. Mental and physical journeys are launched by desire.

Desire! I inhaled and looked around me. Desire was everywhere in evidence: for safe passage, for family ties, for good weather, for comfort, for music, for cheap gas. Then my aperture of desire widened to include my desire to share the exhilaration of discovery that my ecological contemplations had awarded me. Minds and senses may find comfort in familiarity, but they soar in the presence of newness.

Newness! Newness was all around me, yet the scene surrounding me seemed more oppressive than exhilarating. Newness was apparent in the cell phone upgrade, the car seat for the new baby that replaced the seat used by the older child, the battery-operated sneakers on the 4-year-old that lit up with every step, the spill-proof coffee mug on the dashboard, the digital camera in the trunk, and the deluxe dog collar made from double thick premium nylon. I imagined our van being commandeered by a band of masked environmental Robin Hoods who confiscated our luxuries and left us bereft along the highway. But this hardship would not last long. A single trip to any mall in any town between "here" and "there" could replace it all. I sighed. What force was directing the acquisition habits of the intelligent, kind-hearted, well-meaning people in this van? I searched for visible evidence of this invisible power.

Power! The power of two hundred and fifty horses was churning under the hood of the van in an area not much bigger than a bread box. How much horsepower was needed to drive our wants so far beyond our needs that necessity was long forgotten? This unnamed power was not an abstraction. I observed. Everything in sight beyond the windshield had been subjected to displays of human power. Paving suppressed growth. Drains channeled water. Signs limited speeds and prohibited littering. Wires directed communications. Conduits distributed energy. A bridge spanned a river. Radar detected speeders. What was the nature of human power? Had human power become nature?

Nature! Tree-covered hills met the cloud-covered sky. Nature everywhere was marked by humans. Weeds along the road enjoyed a banquet of carbon emissions, trees were trimmed to allow clear passage for vehicles, roadbeds were leveled to permit a smooth drive, and banks were contoured for exits and entrances. The sun that shone through yellow-tinged clouds illuminated grazing deer that had grown accustomed to speeding traffic. For miles, strange chunky objects that were black and shiny appeared along the shoulder of the roadway. No, they were not boulders; they were garbage bags filled with litter. I imagined untying them and peering inside. Where did all these discards come from? Was their route from manufacture to litter global?

Globalism! Perhaps I could discern this route by examining the objects in my midst, since they were all potential road litter. I murmured to myself that even a 10-hour drive would not have provided sufficient time to examine the accumulation. The van itself was an emblem of global exchange. The steel was made in Japan, the tires in North Carolina, the chrome in Singapore, the engine in Alabama, the gasoline in Saudi Arabia, the radio in Sweden, the headlights in Georgia, the microchips in the car keys in Texas. I was distressed to envision shipping containers loading cartons onto all the trucks in those far flung ports and depots, spewing exhaust as they headed toward automobile assembly plants. So I decided to focus on a benefit of globalism. Everyone likes diversity.

Diversity! I examined the T-shirts, maps, combs, coins, belts, backpacks, flashlight, and ice scraper around me and imagined the tremendous number of decisions required to assemble this collection. Each item had been selected from a profusion of alternative brands, sizes, colors, qualities, patterns, styles, and so forth. Diversity abounds today in human experience, but there are widespread fears that diversity may be languishing among nonhuman organisms. The race to halt extinctions caused by human indiscretions receives a lot of press. I was curious to seek evidence of human efforts to increase biological diversity. I surveyed this self-contained van as if it were the globe. I smiled. My search was instantly rewarded. The Great Dane sleeping beside me was originally bred for hunting. The apples in the snack pack were hybrids. The corn in the oil that fried the chips was genetically modified. But my smile vanished when I imagined the uncertain effects of our manipulations. My limited vantage point provided dramatic views of unknown outcomes. Even our speeding vehicle must be having an effect upon diversity by depleting oxygen, increasing carbon, heating air, pounding pavement, adding noise, and causing road-kills. Though crows and squirrels seem to be thriving, peregrine falcons and New England cottontails may only survive through acts of mercy.

Mercy! Two out of the four adults in the car were able to enjoy this journey because of advanced medical interventions. I am one of them. Two operations and an ongoing regimen of medicines have postponed my death.

Death! I fixated on the squishes, squashes, and splats accumulating on the windshield that were destined to be scrubbed away at the next gas station. I groaned. From an ecological perspective, this massacre was a waste of good organic nourishment. Vultures and crows provided a more environmentally harmonious sight when we passed them relishing the feasts provided by a road-kill deer, a groundhog, and the sprawled entrails from an unidentifiable carcass. These efficient sanitation crews get little credit for managing wastes and cycling decay.

Decay! Yesterday's half-eaten apple lay moldering on the floor beside scattered Cheerios and raisins dropped by the children during some previous trip. At the same time the carpet was accumulating soil, the dent on the van's fender was generating rust, the tires were becoming brittle, the engine was wearing out, the chrome was forming pits, and the passengers were aging. My deceased mother would have been horrified by the slowly rotting mess. I sighed. She never understood that decay is an essential ingredient of the Earth's vitality and dynamism. To her, decay signaled the need to discard food, replace appliances, and apply another layer of makeup. She never honored it as the intermediary between death and life. These forces conjoin in another marvel she never honored: dirt.

Dirt! The timing was perfect. We arrived at our geographical destination just as I arrived at my mental destination. I squeezed my body between a series of hurdles imposed by pets and adults and children and their respective belongings, stretched my stiff limbs, and happily set foot upon the mantle of the Earth-unpaved, unseeded, unorganized dirt.

My journey passed quickly. I hope you safely complete the journey through the pages of this volume and that you arrive at the end energized to continue the expedition. The ecological interpretations of the themes it addresses are offered as points of departure, not conclusions. They are presented as opportunities for refinement, expansion, interpretation, and implementation. Good wishes and bon voyage.

Acknowledgments

Exploring art within the context of ecology involved harvesting crops of facts and concepts that had already been cultivated by scientists, and aligning them with works of artists who had already integrated much of that information. It was exhilarating to explore their scholarship and creativity, and it is a privilege to share the insights they taught me with my readers. They are the originators of the content that I hope captivates my readers as it captivated me.

The contributions of Skip Schuckmann deserve special mention. He tirelessly explained the complexities of ecosystem dynamics and then demonstrated how the theoretical constructs of ecology can be crafted into an art practice and applied throughout a life practice.

Dr. Dan Franck generously activated his academic credentials to secure the scientific grounding of these textlets. His editing helped assure that the information is not only accurate, but that it is also well articulated.

Andrew Weintraub served as a valued reader whose astute suggestions have significantly affected this text.

Arthur Hoener designed these textlets within restrictions imposed by a simple, black-and-white format. He graciously accepted these limitations and demonstrated the resourcefulness to compose a lively and visually appealing publication.

Cynthia Werthamer went beyond routine copy editing by sharing valuable insights about format and clarity.

Alexandra Tuller and Dean Temple of Drake Creative designed a website that both honored and refined the ecological, philosophical, and design principles of this project.

The artists are not only to be acknowledged for their contributions to this publishing enterprise. More significantly, they should be recognized for their contributions to the culture, which is now wiser and more attentive, and the environment that is strengthened and vitalized by their efforts.

Readers also deserve to be acknowledged. I express my appreciation to you for offering your attention to this textlet.

I am eager to hear your comments.

Linda Weintraub

artnow@juno.com

ECOcentrism

The term ecocentric was invented by me after I searched in vain for a word that
describes humans relating to the nonhuman environment in a
harmonious, respectful, and pragmatic manner. There are 750,000
words in the English language, and I could not find one that provides
this meaning. This verbal omission seemed symptomatic of our cultural
disregard for the environment. It revealed that ecological consciousness
is an orphan concept that is likely to remain unadopted until, at the very
least, it is granted its own word.

Then, to my surprise, I discovered that I shared both the frustration and the solution
with authors on books relating to ethics, philosophy, politics,
management, population, and education. We all noted that the word
anthropocentric was invented to refer to the practice of interpreting
reality exclusively in terms of human values and human experience. It
omits ecological inclusiveness. Likewise, the word egocentric exists
to describe people who care only about themselves and their own
needs. The popularity of this concept is apparent in the many synonyms
it has accumulated. Switching prefixes from 'ego' to 'eco' directs
awareness away from selfish interests and toward ecologically inclusive
considerations. When ecocentric synonyms enter the dictionaries and
minds of English speakers, they will replace the prefix 'ego,' which
means self, with the prefix 'eco,' which means home or habitat.
Synonyms for egocentric include self-absorbed, self-centered, self-
involved, and self-serving. Therefore, synonyms for ecocentric would be
habitat-absorbed, habitat-centered, habitat-involved, and habitat-serving.
It is an adjective that means being focused on ecological relationships.

It seems this new entry in the catalogue of terminologies is symptomatic of the fact
that ecological consciousness is becoming an increasingly powerful
determinant of legislation, economic policies, ethical principles,
business practices, international relations, and urban planning.
Elements of ecological thought are also infiltrating political policies,
manufacturing protocols, lifestyle patterns, and cultural expressions.
Furthermore, ecologies are proliferating across disciplines, which now
comprise behavioral ecology, urban ecology, social ecology, acoustic
ecology, political ecology, industrial ecology, Christian ecology, and
media ecology. Art is participating in this paradigm shift. By embracing
human and nonhuman forms of life, artists are urging egocentric
behaviors into ecocentric alignment with environmental directives. In
this manner they are contributing to the overhaul of cultural values.

The four-billion-year narrative of the emergence of life on Earth discloses the fallacy
of human-centeredness. This chronicle reveals that oxygen, for
example, did not originate exclusively to support human life. The
drama of creation and recreation had been running unabated for
between three and four billion years before Homo sapiens came into
existence approximately 250,000 years ago. Still, we seem fixated on
human-centered perspectives. We commonly honor humanists who
utilize reasoned and critical thinking to promote the self-interest of our

species. The humanities are pursued as a canon of higher education. Humanitarians are recognized for applying their reasoning powers and their education to advance human welfare. In our brief occupation on Earth, we humans have succeeded in trapping, controlling, and processing the sources of energy that first sparked life. We have behaved like commanders of the biosphere when, in truth, it is the biosphere that is indispensable for our survival.

By introducing ecological themes, artists can contribute to a pioneering effort that combines sophisticated technologies with respectful ecologies. You have already mastered the concept of ecological inclusiveness if you can imagine the multifarious ways you are modifying the environment while you are reading the words on this page. Your breathing is altering the oxygen and carbon ratios in the atmosphere. You are subtracting warmth by casting a shadow, but you are adding warmth by emitting calories and by using electric lights. Meanwhile, you are contributing to a change in the Earth's energy supply and air quality if the room in which you are located is temperature-controlled for your comfort. Ecocentric themes provide artists with opportunities to introduce such fundamental considerations and their challenging implications into the public discourse.

ECOscience/ECOart

Since art is a product of free creative expression, and ecology is the science of the relationships between organisms and their environments, creating a partnership between these divergent human pursuits may seem like a formula for dysfunction, not compatibility. Yet this textlet provides evidence of 10 successful joint ventures between ecology and art. Some projects are the product of collaborations between artists and scientists. Other mergers occur within the mind of a single artist. Both approaches take advantage of the fact that human brains are proficient at calculating, intuiting, inventing, investigating, and conducting myriad additional tasks. The brain is also versatile at managing innumerable inputs and coordinating dissimilar functions. Eco-art is interdisciplinary. It acknowledges the multifarious capacities of the human mind. The following statements identify five areas where such cross-fertilizations help assure the vitality of culture and the future of current forms of life.

Merit – Accuracy measures the merit of ecological data. Accuracy can also measure the merits of an art work, but art introduces additional criteria of merit, such as imagination, expressiveness, relevance, aesthetics, skill, persuasiveness, and metaphoric significance.

Outreach – Ecological research and analysis is circulated among specialists and colleagues. Although some ecologists may choose to cross the professional divide as educators and journalists, it is not the responsibility of ecologists to disseminate their findings throughout society. In contrast, outreach is an essential component of art. Thus, art provides the vehicle by which ecological insights can infiltrate culture and become a force of social change.

Method – Ecology's methods and products are essentially impersonal. Artists, however, enjoy the privilege of personalizing their activities by embellishing facts with charm, intimidation, amusement, persuasion, threats, shock, seduction, beauty, and ingenuity. Artists have license to employ all human communicative capacities.

Inquiry – Ecology offers a philosophical and scientific framework to ask: How did it get this way? Art can expand the implications of this question by contemplating: Why did it get this way? Are there other possibilities? Which alternatives are worth pursuing? How can we attain them?

Role – Ecologists are scientists. Artists can be scientists, but they also act as prophets, visionaries, moralists, pragmatists, tricksters, futurists, and revolutionaries.

ECOcentric Topics

If ecocentric art were compared to a food, it would resemble thick aromatic gravy, not a single food like a carrot or milk. Ecocentric art is an art of merger, subtlety, and richness. It has little in common with simplifying distillations and isolating separations. It is comparable to a symphony, an alloy, a conglomerate.

Art conjoins with ecology each time artists synchronize nonhuman organisms, the non-living environment, and human actions. This encompassing mandate revamps, and sometimes reverses, cherished cultural values and entrenched cultural norms. Thus, although all 10 artists and groups discussed in this textlet address conventional concepts, the content is not conventional. Their ecocentric interpretations constitute an exciting, and sometimes daring, arena of artistic exploration. This volume offers the few categories I described in the Preface. They might appear among many others on a vast spreadsheet of thematic opportunities awaiting adoption by eco-artists.

Desire – The Reverend Billy Talen explores how ecocentric consciousness might break the habit of shopping to fulfill desires.

Newness – Rob Fischer demonstrates that our desire for newness might be satisfied by inventing new uses for old stuff.

Power – Superflex directs its own powers to empowering others so that people can manage their own lives and the destinies of their own habitats.

Nature – Dave Burns and Matias Viegener invent an amusing metaphor for the current unnatural state of nature.

Globalism – Shelley Sacks portrays globalism as a network of resource and energy exchange that enriches some populations and their habitats, but depletes other populations and other habitats.

Diversity – Eduardo Kac proposes that diversifying life forms by mixing the genetics of different species enables humans to compensate for species extinctions.

Mercy – Jean Grant demonstrates the biological and psychological drawbacks of mercy, even if it is intended as an act of kindness, by applying the principles of natural selection to plants and to humans.

Death – Catherine Chalmers stages cockroach executions to expose idiosyncratic attitudes toward death that reveal the alienation of contemporary civilization from biology.

Decay – Damien Hirst relishes the mess that follows death but precedes the formation of new life.

Dirt – Joe Scanlan provides a triumphant conclusion to this exploration of ecocentric themes by creating an ecocentric masterpiece – lush, fertile dirt.

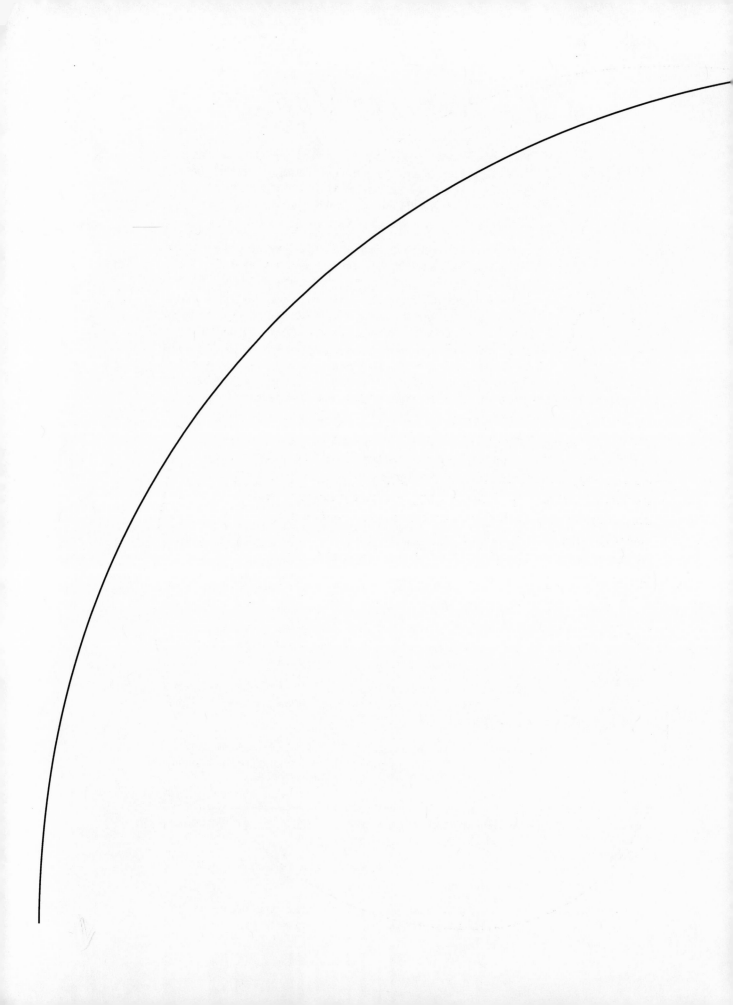

Desire

What do you want right now? To sleep, yawn, scratch, eat, or leave the room? Do your desires politely wait their turns for fulfillment, or are some desires bullies that impose their wills upon your actions and monopolize your attention? If you are reading this book, you are probably familiar with the desire to engage with art. Have you wondered about its origin? Does art represent a need because you cannot survive without it? Or is it a want because you prefer art to other things? Is your desire for art the result of a negative impulse, such as avoiding tedious labor? Or is it a positive impulse, such as pursuing beauty?

Desire: An Ecocentric Interpretation

Positive and negative urges are inherent to animals and plants. Biologists use the term 'tropism' to refer to an organism's involuntary response to a stimulus. For example, cold-blooded reptiles seek sunny ledges; this positive phototropism enables them to warm themselves. Likewise, paramecia shy away from acid; this negative chemotropism protects them from dissolving. Every form of life has its own collection of tropisms that may induce responses to temperature, light, gravity, sound, touch, taste, smell, color, and a host of other sensual phenomena. Tropisms direct the behavior of all forms of life on the planet, including humans. Negative tropisms repel them from life-threatening hazards. Positive tropisms attract them to life-enhancing conditions.

Despite the fact that human infants are born equipped with innate and automatic tropic responses, it would be mistaken to reduce the behaviors of humans to such simplistic reactions. Humans are not like nonhuman life forms that die with the same tropisms they possessed when they were born—even if they've learned new ways to satisfy them. As humans mature, 'built-in' components of behavior are supplemented with 'add-ons.' Our impressionable minds and finicky bodies provide fertile territory for the implantation of desires and aversions that are devised by our imaginations. At the same time, we are susceptible to stimuli that promise to deliver happiness, security, romance, health, and/or adventure, and that pledge to avert pain, loneliness, credit problems, illness, and/or aging.

Some advertisers invent cravings and then urge us to indulge them. Others concoct fears and press us to seek protection from them. They channel both kinds of desires through commerce. Advertisers foster shopping as a hobby, a sport, an entertainment, an opiate, an art form, a national pastime. They encourage us to equate affection with purchased gifts, honor holidays by running sales, and dump our overflow or stash it in self-storage bins so that purchasing can continue unabated. Commercial promoters even capitalize on the frustrations that often accompany such quests for satisfaction. Stress afflicts folks who service their buying habits with consumer credit. Anxiety besets families that maintain their desired living standards with multiple income-earners. Advertisers insist that purchasing another package of consumables will provide relief, not aggravate our problem.

There is another casualty from lifestyles in which glamor, comfort, status, and convenience are derived from material purchases. The environment often bears the brunt of the gathering of resources, their manufacture, their use, and their disposal. The Reverend Billy Talen is attempting to save human souls and secure ecosystem health by overhauling contemporary definitions of delight and aversion. He is summoning the persuasive strategies of evangelical preachers to instill negative tropisms toward excessive purchases, and positive tropisms toward empty closets.

(Figure 0030)

Reverend Billy Talen

Born 1950 Rochester, Minnesota
Franconia College in New Hampshire BA
San Francisco State University MA

The Reverend Billy Talen is a tropic crusader. He has dedicated his career to diminishing the allure of shopping and augmenting the allure of restraint. Talen is a performance artist who transmits evangelical entreaties against consumerism with the fervor of a Baptist preacher and the authority of a religious doctrine. His sermons are delivered in soaring, rhythmic verses that erupt into exuberant exclamations of "Hallelujah!" and "Praise be to God!" and "Amen!"

Talen is the self-appointed reverend in a church of his own devising. It is called the Church of Stop Shopping. His frequent admonitions—that to "save your soul" you must "back away from that silly little product on the shelf"—are accompanied by the surging gospel harmonies of the Stop Shopping Choir. Golden-robed members don't merely raise their voices on high. They can barely contain the zeal of becoming born-again Stop-Shoppers. They jump. They stomp. They cheer. They clap.

Meanwhile, sweat trickles down Talen's radiant face. His Elvis-like pompadour bops across his forehead as he gazes upward to heaven and scowls downward toward hell. Dressed in a polyester leisure suit with an ecclesiastical collar, he may present an amusing spectacle, but he delivers a compelling message. The contagion of Talen's evangelical vision sweeps art world sophisticates who are amused by his satire. But it also enraptures more homespun folks who are inspired by his passion.

Talen's vision of paradise consists of idyllic communities untainted by corporate empires. For this reason, current shoppers are targets of the church's mission, converted shoppers comprise its congregation, and shopping sites serve as its pulpits. Although Reverend Billy sometimes preaches in museums, theaters, churches, and universities, he and his band of faithful followers spread the Word most affectively in Starbucks, the Disney Store, GAP, Wal-Mart, Barnes and Noble, and Nike. These epicenters of conspicuous consumption serve as staging grounds for Church of Stop Shopping events. 'Spat theater,' for example, is a staged drama in which members of the choir pose as customers and pretend to argue about the ethics of consumption. Revival meetings are orchestrated in these sites to proclaim the joys of nonconsumerism. Flash mobs are staged with hundreds of supporters who convene in a particular location and recite into their cell phones, in unison, the First Amendment, protecting the right to freedom of religion and freedom of expression. On other occasions the choir goes among the people, duct-taping over Nike swooshes, Levi's tags, and other evidence of offending consumerism that those people are wearing. The church observes Buy Nothing Day, a national holiday that sanctifies a reverse-merchandising theology. The Reverend also conducts exorcisms upon the iconic representations of sinful consumption, such as cash registers and credit cards. On one occasion the entire choir spent the day at a Wal-Mart store, silently pushing empty shopping carts up and down the aisles. These events

(Figure 0031)

typically culminate in the choir's spirited rendition of the "Stop Shopping! Stop Shopping!" hymn. The Reverend has been arrested on numerous occasions. Evidently it is illegal to not shop in America.

On one occasion, the Church of Stop Shopping conducted a service in which the Reverend took a shiny Sunbeam toaster and put it in the center of the altar. A young man named Jonah walked up the aisle of the church. Witnesses report that Jonah's admiration for the shiny appliance was apparent. Still, he willingly submitted to the rite of exorcism that promised to release him from his material addictions. The essay entitled "Shopper, Repent!"[1] not only provides a vivid account of this event, it summarizes the extensive repertoire of desire-altering techniques employed by Reverend Billy and his choir. These strategies are identified before each paragraph of the Reverend's text.

Encouragement: *"The congregation prayed that he (Jonah) would somehow not grab that sleek chrome bread heater (it resembled a Mercedes coupe and had computerized controls, including a woman's voice that purred 'Your toast is done'). I placed my hand on the forehead of this shaking soul ... As Jonah reached for the product we prayed hard. The choir hummed and the deacons moved forward to lay hands on the craven consumer as the devil pulled the young man's begging fingers toward the toaster. ... But wait! Jonah's hand hesitated, and then pulling out of that force field, it flew back and wavered there in the air. Jonah stared, in shock, at his released fingers."*

Liberation: *"Then he ran around the church as if proving to a Pentecostal TV audience that now he could walk. Held aloft by the preacher, his hand was shaking with new freedom, unburdened. The Stop Shopping Gospel Choir was swaying with the power of a receiptless God-Goddess that surpasseth all valuation. The object looked cheated, cuckolded. Finally the Sunbeam deluxe toaster was just fucking junk."*

Warning: *"Not buying is a brave thing to do. At first it may induce vertigo, identity weirdness, and a desire for an unwanted pregnancy, but most often a new believer will have an abnormal kitsch-acquisition fit. The first response to the break in buying may be a huge sucking sound in your hands–you want to buy something, anything. You are headed for a relapse, a spree. My pastoral advice is to steer clear of Ralph Lauren, Kenneth Cole, or any other fashion designer who is trying to anticipate the not-buying revolution by copping a look of weatheredness, offhandedness, or lack of manufacture. Their sales departments think all day about your escape, admiring it and blocking it. They study you via surveillance feeds as they sit in their easy chairs, thoughtfully rubbing their chins."*

Wonder: *"When you lift your hand from the product and back away from it, a bright, unclaimed space opens up. Consumers think it is a vacuum. It is really only the unknown–full of suppressed ocean life, glitterati from Bosch, DNA twists, and childhood quotes that, if remembered, would burn down the Disney Store. Many Americans consider this withdrawing* gesture a dark thing. Officially, it is absurd, an anti-gesture, like an American who didn't go west, who didn't go into space, who had sex without a car."

Courage: "In the Church of Stop Shopping we believe that buying is not nearly as interesting as not-buying. When you back away from the purchase, the product may look up at you with wanton eyes, but it will slump quickly back onto the shelf and sit there trying to get a life. The product needs you more than you need it—remember that."

Resolve: "Now, if you try this—if you lift your hand from the product, pull that hand back into the aisle, back away from the product, and carefully move toward the door—you may feel turbulence deep in your muscles' memory. You may feel the old grab, the lift, the swipe of plastic, and finally the bagging for the road. The ex-consumer can easily lose his or her footing, buffeted by all those ghost gestures."

Remorse: "Like crack cocaine or membership in the National Rifle Association, shopping is an annihilating addiction that must be slowed down to be stopped, or flooded with new and different light. But people, please—do something! Think of something quick. The research phase is over. How many times do we have to hear that 7 percent of the world's population is taking a third of the world's resources? How many neighborhoods need to be malled? When will our foreign policy be violent enough to turn our heads?"

Determination: "Recently a local Starbucks rang with shouts of 'We are from the Church of the Necessary Interruption!'. We try many strategies. Enacting a purchase in a formal church ritual on Sunday or acting out a comic version of being born again might help those parishioners when they are cornered in Temptation Mall. Sweatshops are truly shocking, and I've seen the sheer force of the information stop a shopper. We make dramas, we sing and shout, and chain ourselves to Mickey Mouse. We are desperate to access the bright and unclaimed space that the corporations must desperately hide."

Sympathy: "In another time, long, long ago, maybe you could have gone ahead and had a life without shopping. But now life without shopping is something that takes years of practice, since shopping is so virulent and ubiquitous that mothers are bathing their wombs with sounds of Mozart so that their fetuses will score higher on their SATs. Now everything from the most intimate disease to daydreaming is a pretext for the avant-fascism of convenience, comfort, and closure."

Willpower: "We might call that unclaimed space 'ordinary life.' And how do we design that back in? How much of real life hasn't made it into our fully mediated consumption? Can we ever go home again? We have made thousands of purchases—thousands of times the doors have closed behind us as we walked farther into that big, big sale."

Enticement: "The bumper sticker says Birth, Shopping, Death. Well, birth and death are a part of ordinary life. And ordinary life is itself amazing; the intriguing mystery that precedes birth and follows death does not stop when we are alive. Perhaps the great con began when churches made us pay for(?) our own arrival and departure. Life itself has as much unknown in it as death; it is just as inexplicable. That's the thrill of the ride. We say, 'Put the ODD Back in God!'"

Reassurance: "We shop because we fear life. We shop because we want to banish from life something we identify with death, the unknown. It waits for us in that bright, unclaimed space. Of course, we are trained to think of what we can't know as a bad thing. Actually, it is the source of the brightness; it is why this space has no owner."

Promise: "I'm claiming that the rejection of living-by-products opens up a sensual and peopled life, and it also has in it an acceptance of the unknown, which is always waiting with the glorious indifference of the fires that float above us in the night sky. Is it a contradiction that accepting this unknown is what makes it possible for us to live together? Well, there is nothing more thoroughly mysterious than love, thank God. Those who organize defenses against the Unknown (such as religious fundamentalists and consumer fundamentalists) foment numbness, hatred, and war. Unfortunately, they have perfected their imitation of ordinary living, and that comes to us as the comforting ghost gesture of shopping."

Suspense: "Ordinary life will feel counterintuitive, to put it mildly. But what will happen to the American consumer when the consuming stops is about as fascinating a question as we can ask."

Reverend Billy enumerated 14 strategies of human persuasion. He did not invent them. They are among the many strategies familiar to successful advertisers, public relations specialists, politicians, religious leaders, educators, and other influencers of human behavior. The Reverend demonstrates how they can be used to foster ecocentric values.

(Figure 0030)   Reverend Billy Talen, St. Marks Church, March, 2005, 7 x 5 inches, Nikon D1X Digital Camera TIFF file, Courtesy Fred Askew, Photography Fred Askew

(Figure 0031)   Reverend Billy Talen, Old South MeetingMeeting House, Boston, MA, April, 2005, 7 x 5 inches, Nikon D1X Digital Camera TIFF file, Courtesy Fred Askew, Photography Fred Askew

Full Color images and supplemental images at www.Avant-Guardians.com

Exploring Desire

1. Reverend Billy Talen takes a full-throttled approach to behavior modification. His zeal to reform consumers drives him to package his moralistic lessons in soul-stirring songs and verse. The following artists utilize very different tactics than those used by Talen, but their works aspire to a similar goal. Song Dong quietly presents a radical alternative to consumerism by honoring nonmaterialistic values. The Center for Land Use Interpretation rejects both Talen's hyperbole and Dong's subtlety. It prefers to orchestrate direct encounters between its audience and the often grim industrial underpinnings of consumerist lifestyles.

   Song Dong's *Writing diary with water* (1995–present) refers to a daily practice in which Dong sits with a particular block of stone, lifts a calligraphy brush, dips the brush in water, and writes a diary entry on the surface of the stone. In seconds, the text vanishes without a trace. In another performance entitled *Stamping the water* (1996) that Dong conducted in the Lhasa River in Tibet, he repeatedly stamped the sacred water using an archaic wooden seal carved with the character for water. As with his invisible water diary, the stamping gesture left no trace. Likewise, to create *Breathing* (1996), Dong lay stretched out, face down, in Tiananmen Square until his condensed breath formed a layer of ice on the cold paving stones. When the ice melted, evidence of the work evaporated. Although photographs record these pieces, the performances proceeded from impulse to memory without leaving a trace.

   The Center for Land Use Interpretation (CLUI) conducts its art practice as a research organization that studies human interactions with the Earth's surface. These efforts are presented as art works to enlighten the public. Conducting guided public bus tours is one way it accomplishes this mission. Because the CLUI promotes these educational field trips as hip art events, people clamor for tickets. One trip (2005) brought 50 passengers to Terminal Island, the hub of the Los Angeles and Long Beach ports in California. Together they comprise the third largest port in the world. Billions of dollars' worth of furniture, clothing, appliances, toys, office supplies, food, cosmetics, and vehicles made and/or processed abroad arrive in 8-by-8-by-40-foot freight containers. Passengers on the CLUI tour bus got a behind-the-scenes view of congested stacks of boxcar containers that stretched as far as the eye could see.

   A. Create two works of art that address the same common desire. Choose one that is damaging to the environment such as drinking bottled water.

      a. Employ a different strategy to diminish this desire in each work of art. You may adopt strategies used by the Reverend Billy: warning, wonder, courage, resolve, remorse, determination, sympathy, willpower, enticement, reassurance, promise, suspense, encouragement, and liberation.

b. Present these art works to acquaintances or strangers and then interview these people to determine which strategy is more likely to alter their behavior.

B. Imagine a bus trip to the 520-store complex known as the Mall of America, where every year 40 million shoppers (roughly eight times the population of the state of Minnesota, where the mall is located) make purchases. Now imagine that a detour was planned by Song Dong as an art event.

a. Where might he take the passengers?

b. What might happen there?

c. How do you think the passengers would respond?

C. Imagine a bus trip to the Mall of America organized by the Center for Land Use Interpretation.

a. Which three locations would the CLUI choose to visit in order to enlighten the passengers about the personal and/or environmental problems associated with extreme consumerism? Would it include Nordstrom, Sears, the 14-screen movie theater, Camp Snoopy amusement park, Underwater Adventure Aquarium, wedding chapel, Mall of America campus of National American University, Lego Imagination Center, River Church at the Mall of America, parking lot, loading dock, dumpster area, or some other location?

b. Explain your selections.

2. Examine your motives and select two strong desires (positive tropisms) and two strong aversions (negative tropisms). Answer the following questions as they apply to each desire and each aversion:

Is it inherent or a product of socialization?

Is it necessary or expendable?

Is this desire or avoidance something you share with many people?

Is its intensity minor or extreme?

Is its expected time of delivery immediate or eventual?

Is it easy or difficult to fulfill or avoid?

Is recurrence rare, sporadic, or frequent?

Is the effect long-term or short-term?

Is the effect permanent or temporary?

Is fulfillment or avoidance a matter of luck, will, skill, ingenuity, money, other?

Is the environmental cost of satisfaction or avoidance significant or minimal?

If the desire is frustrated or the aversion occurs, will you try again, replace it, discard it?

A. Create a work of art that reflects these personal desires and aversions. You may use any medium and any manner of expression.

B. Examine this work as if it described someone else, not you. Write your estimate of this person's current contentment, potential for future contentment, and changes to current behaviors that might improve future contentment.

3. The first part of this exercise invites you to examine your personal impulse to engage art. The second part addresses the effect of art on your desires and aversions. The third part explores the influence of your art work upon your audience.

A. Answer the following questions:

Where did my desire for art experiences originate?

Does art represent a need because I cannot survive without it?

Is it a want because I prefer art to other things?

Is my desire for art the result of a negative impulse, such as avoiding tedious labor?

Is my desire for art a positive impulse, such as pursuing beauty?

B. Discuss a specific art work that has had a strong effect upon you. Did this art work reinforce your current values, introduce a new desire or aversion, suppress an existing desire or aversion, or influence you in some other way? Did the theme, the style, the size, the medium, and/or some other component account for its effect?

C. Explain how you would like your art work to affect your audience. Would you like to reinforce a current value, introduce a new desire or aversion, suppress an existing desire or aversion, or have another kind of influence?

D. Create a work of art based upon a common consumer habit. This is the work's theme. Describe how you intend to affect this habit. This is the work's intention. How might you accomplish this goal? This is the work's strategy.

4. Ecological considerations suggest the need to overhaul definitions of delight by associating them with frugality, discretion, restraint, and practicality. Create or describe an art work that summons the persuasive strategies of a specific advertisement to instill desires to compost, or recycle, or conserve.

---

(1) Billy Talen, "Shopper, Repent!" SoMA Review, January 11, 2005. http://www.somareview.com/revbilly.cfm

Newness

"What's new?" This familiar question can be answered in two ways. It can either elicit a report on recent events, such as "I just graduated," or it can offer definitions of concepts of newness. The word "new" can mean recent, never used, just discovered, novel, unfamiliar, additional, rejuvenated, latest, fashionable, and so forth. In the context of this essay, new refers to the replacement of serviceable items and ideas. Improved performance is a practical motive that frequently activates such exchanges of old for new. But desires for newness are also stirred by impractical urges, such as susceptibility to trends, marketing appeals, or indicators of status.

Newness: An Ecocentric Interpretation

Newness that refers to the replacement of serviceable items and ideas is neither always bad nor always good. The environmental consequences of each instance must be evaluated against the merits of each individual's desire to complete the transition. The following questions present an ecological cost/benefit analysis that readers can apply to both necessities and amusements.

Will my current dissatisfaction be diminished by this new item?

Will it make me happier, healthier, richer, wiser, calmer, more popular

How long will this satisfaction last?

What are the effects of this new item upon neighboring animals and plants.

What are its effects upon animals and plants where it was grown, mined, and/ or manufactured?

What are the environmental costs of this item's packaging and delivery?

What will be the final disposition of this new item when it becomes obsolete?

How many resources were expended to convince me to acquire it?

Does attention to this item distract me from issues that are more important?

A broad range of themes awaits artists who choose to reassess the practice of habitual updates and avoidable replacements. These thematic considerations might also be expressed by journalists and educators. But the message gains significance when it is delivered by an artist. This is because art's long heritage displays a progression of masters using new materials to create new styles and found new movements. When newness is rejected from art, artists relinquish a traditional attribute of their profession. This bold reversal of a core art principle suggests that if newness is being challenged in art, perhaps it should be challenged throughout culture.

Eco-artists are among those who suspect that the taste for newness may be sending the human race on a collision course with the consequences of its own behaviors. These artists are evaluating addictions to quick turnover, built-in obsolescence, fashions, fads, trends, and updates. They are asking, has blind faith in the quest for newness blinded us to its risks? This kind of query can be applied to the annual redesign of automobiles, computer programs, cell phone services, and myriad other phenomena. It can consist of the interrogation of the environmental costs of cordless, rechargeable bug wands that replace the humble flyswatter by suctioning up insects. Other thematic opportunities can arise when artists offer solutions. By originating schemes to improve efficiency, reduce energy consumption, enhance recycling, minimize effluents, artists can demonstrate ways to invigorate environments instead of depleting them.

Rob Fischer does not assume that anything that is new is better than anything that already exists, he assumes that there is advantage in reusing things that are considered out-worn, out-grown, out-of-date, or out-of-style. Fischer is an advocate of recycling. Many artists support this signature axiom of the Green Movement by creating art works with materials they scavenge from wastebaskets, dumpsters, and landfills. They bring items 'in' that others have thrown 'out'. Fischer is special. He recycles his own unsold artworks.

Rob Fischer

Born 1968 Minneapolis, Minnesota
1993 Minneapolis College of Art and Design, interdisciplinary studies

When a manufactured commodity is removed from its protective packaging, gleaming and pristine, it is assigned the status of being new. This is a fragile condition that only persists until the item transitions into a worthless discard, sometimes completing this transition in less time than it takes to create it. At this point, the item is often relegated to a dump or landfill. Rob Fischer introduces an alternative scenario. Even as he is creating a sculpture, he acknowledges that the destiny of all material substances is ultimately to be absorbed and reused by an ecosystem. He manifests this principle by reusing parts of his own sculptures to fabricate new sculptures. Because he has a very respectable sales record, this practice cannot be attributed to financial necessity. Accepting transience as a renewable opportunity, not a terminus, is his willful artistic strategy. Such cannibalizing of his works of art emulates an ecosystem's cyclic patterns of material reuse, a cycle that artists typically resist.

Fischer's sculptures are usually exhibited at conventional venues such as galleries and museums. If they are sold, they are cared for according to typical art protocols. If, however, they are not sold, he takes them apart and utilizes the pieces in future sculptural contexts. Like the reusable components of ecosystems, Fischer's unsold sculptures are constantly being dismantled and re-mantled. They first become less organized. Then they assume a new form as a new sculpture. Configurations are new, but not the materials. As within ecosystems, evolution occurs. Fischer's art works not only persist, they remain active and responsive. In this way Fischer shares an essential attribute of forests and prairies and oceans—he never has a storage problem and he never has to contend with waste.

Fischer reuses the derelict parts of airplanes, trailers, silos, houses, and boats to construct sculptures that resemble an odd assortment of habitats: shacks, lean-tos, cabins, ice-fishing huts, greenhouses, and trailers. All are architectural equivalents of temporary states of being. The provisional status of these types of buildings is augmented by the sculptures' semi-ramshackle appearances. These art works don't wait to age. In fact, their decrepit state is evident as they are being created. Even the armatures that support the structures are rusted and scarred. In this way they reveal a former use. They are emphaticallly not new. Furthermore, Fischer's architectural sculptures are precariously supported on jacks, oil drums, and concrete blocks. These makeshift foundations infer that the structures have been uprooted from previous locations. At the same time, they convey the impression that they will soon be relocated to other sites. Thus, the sculptures introduce two time frames that bracket newness: histories and prospects. They announce their intermediate status. Transience prevails.

In addition to rejecting the aesthetic associated with the pristine qualities of new items, Fischer dismisses the processes responsible for the production of new items that abound in the marketplace. For example, he rejects carefully engineered designs that guarantee predictable outcomes. Instead he utilizes the haphazard rigging inherent to improvised shelters. In order to convey his adoption of the principle of infinite extension, Fischer has been known to place his creative process on display, continuing construction throughout the duration of an exhibition, in full view of observers.

In 2001 Fischer transposed his sculptural practice to the backyard that had served him as an outdoor workspace. He used the site to create a walled garden. Fischer identifies the reconfiguration of this space as "one of

his most significant pieces."[2] Like his sculptures, the garden both utilizes materials from unsold sculptures and supplies materials for ongoing sculptural projects. However, he no longer limits himself to industrial scrap. Live plants enter the arena of sculptural recycling. Dynamic organic systems actually infiltrate his sculptures. Growth manifests the fact that there is no single, definitive condition of being new. All states are temporary.

(Figure 0032)

Thirty Yards is the title of Rob Fischer's contribution to the 2004 Biennial at the Whitney Museum of American Art. The glass-walled dumpster that he constructed is uncharacteristically scrubbed and neatly packed with furniture, house parts, and pieces from old sculptures. Nonetheless, dumpsters suggest debris. Fischer used this prestigious exhibition as an opportunity to reuse parts of the pumping system that feeds his backyard swamp. The swamp system supplied the copper pipe that circulates water through the dumpster sculpture. It is also the source of the leaves that are attached to the sculpture. In addition, seven sculptures were scavenged to construct the art work. Fischer announced this essential component of his art practice by placing a list of the sculptures that supplied the parts on the outside wall where the name of the dumpster company would ordinarily be placed. Fischer refers to this text as a poem. In this manner, the piece conveyed its own history. He explains, "It told about the seven major pieces it contained. All involved tragic events. For example, there was a crushed boat that I had worked on for seven years and abandoned. Then there was the greenhouse which had floorboards taken from an old sculpture."

Although critics praised *Thirty Yards*, Fischer did not sell the sculpture. He comments, "That disappointed me. I liked it as it was. I asked myself if this was the end of the line or if this sculpture should be recycled too."

Fischer resolved the quandary when he chose to reuse crumpled metal that formerly appeared in the Whitney Biennial dumpster to construct *Abstract Sculpture* (2004–05). Then Fischer expanded his own artistic mandate by recycling a piece of his backyard swamp into an indoor sculpture entitled *Summary (Goodyear Ecology)* (2004–05). To create this work he actually transposed his backyard ecosystem to the gallery setting. The excavated muddy tire track and its surrounding live grasses continued to evolve indoors. The grow lights and circulating water that keep the grasses alive are part of the sculpture. This art work was never brand new, and it will never achieve a final state. Growth continues. Death occurs. Mud settles. Fischer weaves entropy and regeneration into his art system.

Fischer did not originally relate his garden to the rest of his sculptural practice. This idea evolved in the same manner that his sculptures evolve. The following narrative reveals how he gradually welcomed biological encroachment as an example of the continuous recycling of materials and the provisional nature of all ecological conditions. Fischer explains, *"My studio used to be an auto repair shop. The building and the yard were full of car parts, a bunch of engines, tires, and clumps of gravel that were solidified from oil that was drained onto the gravel. I moved in and started cleaning. I took hundreds of tires to a recycling place. The scrap metal dealer took all the steel. Nothing was green. The only living form was rats."*

Purged of these unwanted items, Fischer then surveyed the yard that appeared to be empty, except for some sculptures. He was searching for art materials. His first decision was to retain rain on site so that the moisture might coax out invisible forms of life. This policy proved to be so successful that the weeds not only sprouted and grew; they encroached upon his stored sculptures. Fischer acquiesced to the plant invasion and allowed his sculptures to disappear under the growth.

"When the yard was cleared I dug out clumps of gravel. It left lots of holes. I decided they would make perfect ponds. Then I decided to turn the ponds into a swamp. I began to construct a mocked-up version of what would happen in this yard, naturally, over a long time if humans vacated it. I built a tank inside my studio. It was connected to the nine different ponds out in the yard by pipes that were suspended from my sculptures that were housed there. They were part of a machine trying to maintain a swamp by continually pumping water from the lowest pond to the top one. The tank inside was the heart of the system. The water that flowed back out came through an industrial pipe. It looked like it was draining wastewater, but actually the water was very clean because it had been filtered by the swamp. The flowers simply grow. None were planted. They are all weeds. Most of the grasses I dug up from different parts of the city, especially near construction sites where there were piles of dirt."

The constructed swamp demonstrated the power of biotic recycling and the resilience of life. Indeed, Fischer watched, day by day, as the plants overwhelmed his art works. He comments, *"My swamp is not only starting to take over formerly abused land; it is growing across my sculptures. The grasses and the swamp are claiming space from me. I created the swamp's life-support system at the expense of my own sculptures. My sculptures serve as supports for growth. As they decompose, they provide nutrients for plants. It makes my yard totally useless as a work space. Turning this place into a swamp is about destroying my own sculptures. But this swamp is beautiful. Incredible flowers are growing out of nowhere. The swamp works metaphorically, because it is both destructive and hindering and it is beautiful and contemplative."*

Fischer's swamp introduces the never-ending newness of ecosystems that contrasts with the finite newness that characterizes most human manufacturing and art making. Responsiveness to evolving opportunities replaces a rigid adherence to original intentions. The significance of these practices extends far beyond Fischer's art practice. He explains how they have come to guide his life by commenting; *"Now the swamp serves a new use. To me, it relates to constant questioning. Did I make the right choice? What shall we do with our histories? It involves the process of change and death and rebirth and recycling on a personal level. These issues are universal. This is not necessarily ecological or political. It is a metaphor for the process of life choices people make. There are always parts that are accepted and other parts that are rejected."* The following quote by the artist was saved for last because it embodies the future prospect for his evolving swamp sculpture: *"I think some day I will recycle my swamp into a suburban lawn."*

(Figure 0033)

(Figure 0032)   *Rob Fischer, Thirty Yards, 2003, Mixed media, 54 by 174 by 80 inches ,*
                             Courtesy Cohan and Leslie, New York
(Figure 0033)   *Rob Fischer, Panorama of Marsh in Yard, 2004, Courtesy Cohan and Leslie, New York*
Full Color images and supplemental images at www.Avant-Guardians.com

Exploring Newness

Rob Fischer challenges the popular expectation that novelty and newness are associated with progress, and that conservation and reuse are associated with stagnation. Jim Shaw (1952–) and Mike Bidlo (1953–) apply this general edict to art by reusing their predecessors' artistic achievements. Both artists refuse to invent their own images. In fact, the titles of their works announce their rejection of original creation. They defy the assumption that newness is a prerequisite of merit in art.

Jim Shaw's painting exhibition at the prestigious Institute of Contemporary Arts in London in 2000 was described by an influential critic as "awful, indefensible, crapulous. They are inept, stomach-turning and banal… Is it a painting or a tray of globby mucus? AAARGH!"[2] It is very possible that Shaw was not offended by this declaration. In fact, he might even have agreed, since he did not paint the works of art that were described with such contempt. His exhibition was drawn from his voluminous collection of junked art works he had purchased in thrift stores. Shaw started collecting these works in the 1970s, never paying more than $35 for an original painting. Each time he exhibits the collection, it is arranged according to his personal system of assigning genres: beefcake and cheesecake, psycho, modern art, teenage fantasy and so on. It is the entire collection, not the individual paintings, which constitute his art work. In addition to presenting a catalogue of the ineptitudes and obsessions of unaccomplished artists, the collection reveals that it is not necessary to create new paintings to make an artistic statement.

Mike Bidlo pays homage to acknowledged 20th-century masterworks and, at the same time, violates a hallowed code of art ethics. He accomplishes this double feat by copying works by such renowned masters as Jackson Pollock, Giorgio de Chirico, Andy Warhol, Pablo Picasso, Georgia O'Keeffe, and especially Marcel Duchamp. The titles of Bidlo's works proclaim that these are presented as copies, not forgeries. In each case the word 'not' precedes the copied artist's name. In 2005 Bidlo mounted a new series based upon an infamous act by Robert Rauschenberg that has become a legend in chronicles of 20th-century art. In 1953, Rauschenberg erased an authentic drawing by the renowned abstract expressionist painter Willem de Kooning. Bidlo repeated this audacious artistic act by copying a de Kooning drawing and titling it *NOT de Kooning: Drawing*. Then Bidlo erased his copy of the de Kooning drawing and titled this work *NOT Robert Rauschenberg: Erased de Kooning Drawing*. He brandished his double challenge by exhibiting the accumulated erasure residue and a DVD documenting the process. Bidlo treats existing art as a resource for recycling instead of an object for preservation.

1. The following projects invite you to adopt other artists' concepts.

    A. Apply Rob Fischer's material approach to recycling by reusing something you made to create a work of art.

B. Emulate Jim Shaw's method of art making by gathering and displaying many examples of a commercial object that continually gets redesigned and updated (computer programs, food, clothing, cell phone services, etc.). You may present actual objects, advertisements for these objects, or any other representation of them.

C. Copy Mike Bidlo's conspicuous recycling of the achievements of his predecessors, an artistic approach that is also used among tribute bands. Present your imitation without apology, shame, embarrassment, or deception.

D. Discuss how you feel about being asked to create a work of art by imitating another artist's strategy.

2. Instead of criticizing the wasteful aspects of people's quest for the newest offering in the market, create a work of art that proposes a scheme to improve efficiency, reduce energy consumption, and/or encourage recycling.

3. Determining whether to replace or update an item requires examining the value systems that drive one's own decision making. Conduct an ecological cost/benefit analysis for one labor-saving device or one amusement that you have recently acquired by asking yourself the following questions that were posed at the start of this chapter, now also being recycled:

Was I satisfied before this new item was introduced?

Were my dissatisfactions diminished by this new item?

Did it make me happier, healthier, richer, wiser, calmer, more popular, or more beautiful?

How long did this satisfaction last?

What are the effects of this new item upon animals and plants in my neighborhood?

What are its effects upon animals and plants where it was grown, mined, and/or manufactured?

What are the environmental costs of this item's packaging and delivery?

What will be the final disposition of this new item when it becomes old or obsolete?

How many resources were expended to convince me to acquire it?

Does attention to this item distract me from issues that are more important?

(1) All quotes based on an interview with the artist, September 2004.
(2) Searle, Adrian. "A hundred bucks and all this could be yours... But why on earth would you want it?" The Guardian Unlimited, September 26, 2000.

Power

Like every organism, humans are primarily interested in sustaining themselves and members of their own species. Self-involvement is a biological imperative. This maxim helps to explain why people who are self-motivated, self-reliant, and even self-serving usually enjoy self-respect and also the respect of others. In many cultures these qualities serve as goals of education, measures of good parenting, criteria for effective citizenship, and indicators of economic productivity. They also provide the ethical foundation of legal systems that protect individuals' claims to their own creativity and intelligence through a system of patenting, trademarking, and copyrighting. It is no wonder that self-help industries flourish while self-sacrifice efforts languish. As individuals and as a species, humans excel at self-empowerment.

GUARANÁ POWER is an energy softdrink produced by a guaraná farmers co-operative from Maués in the Brazilian Amazon, in collaboration with Superflex. The farmers have organised themselves in response to the activities of the multinational corporations ▮▮▮▮ and ▮▮▮▮▮, a cartel whose monopoly on the purchase of the raw material has driven the price of guaraná berries down 80%, while the cost of their products to the consumer has risen.

GUARANÁ POWER employs global brands and their strategies as raw material for a counter-economic position while reclaiming the original use of the Maués guaraná plant as a powerful natural tonic, not just a symbol.

GUARANÁ POWER contains original Maués guaraná for energy and empowerment.

For more information: www.guaranapower.org

(Figure 0034

Power: An Ecocentric Interpretation

In addition to personal assertions of power, Homo sapiens pursues the self-interests of the species. Humanity's power to serve its own needs and comforts escalates as we increase our ability to capture and command the Earth's energetic resources, and apply them to the Earth's material resources. In ancient times, fingernails, teeth, fingers, and tongues comprised the anatomical tool chest that performed every life-sustaining function. Humanity might have remained dependent upon this modest set of tools were it not for human cognition, which soon began augmenting humanity's tool kit. The mind's observant faculties discovered sticks and stones. Then its analytic faculties developed mechanics, levers, screws, gears, wheels, and pulleys. As time went by, its imaginative faculties conceived of ways to augment power by employing cattle, water wheels, windmills, steam engines, internal combustion engines, electric motors, jet engines, rocket science, nuclear reactors, and nanotechnologies.

Over time the human species gained the capacity to dictate when and how nonhuman life-forms, the nonliving environment, and other humans should be used for our well-being. We are unique among all species in our ability to dominate all three of these components of our environment. We determine which trees are felled by the logger's ax, which endangered plants are protected, which mineral deposits are depleted, which animals are coddled as pets and which are slaughtered as meat. We influence weather patterns, water states, air quality, species diversity, soil conditions, and land topography.

We already excel at firing the machines that rumble in factories, churn up the land, tame the waters, and soar through the atmosphere. But when these triumphs of human accomplishment are viewed within environmental contexts, questions arise:

Will the human exertion of power help or hinder our descendants?

What is the optimal ratio between assuring our survival and seeking our pleasure?

Now that we have mastered the use of horsepower, can we master the power of love?

SUPERFLEX is not sitting around contemplating these issues; it is not waiting for a consensus of opinion to direct its efforts; it is not expecting to be hired; it never asks for permission. This enterprising art group is proactive in its effort to empower weak humans and weak ecosystems.

SUPERFLEX

Jakob Fenger
Born 1968 Denmark
Royal Danish Academy of Fine Arts

Rasmus Nielsen
Born 1969 Denmark
Royal Danish Academy of Fine Arts

Bjørnstjerne Christiansen
Born 1969 Denmark
Royal Danish Academy of Fine Arts

Superpowers are entities that possess so much authority they can force their will upon powerful entities as well as weak ones. Superpowers can coerce. They have the ability to oppress.

The term "super" is included in the name of this group of artists, chosen to exemplify the theme of power. Yet the term "superpower" can only be used in this essay as a dramatic contrast to the values this Danish art group upholds. The quality that SUPERFLEX displays in all their projects is super-flexibility. SUPERFLEX is flexible about selecting areas of engagement throughout the world. It is flexible about collaborators, mediums, and topics. But it is strict about adhering to its mission. Power enters their work not as a self-aggrandizing scheme, but as a generous offering to people who are relatively defenseless and ecosystems that are faltering. Instead of coveting power for themselves, the members of SUPERFLEX seek ways to achieve more equitable economic distribution, broader democratic representation, and more sustainable environmental conditions.

Even art qualifies as a form of cultural domination when it supports superstar status and elitism. SUPERFLEX explains, "There seems to be an analogy between the art system and the world of politics: only a few powerful individuals decide about the course of policies, rules and values. The art system is one of the last citadels of archaic conservatism and incestual practice in the way it is organized and functions."[1]

SUPERFLEX introduces an alternative based upon generosity. Instead of monopolizing production and seeking adulation, the group produces opportunities for others to assert their power. Its art works resemble verbs for conducting work, not nouns for display and preservation. Their entire art practice is an offering of tools. This distinctive mission is explained in the *SUPERFLEX/ Tools Book:* "The tools invite people to do something: to become active. Tools are framed by and shaped in specific social and local situations and generate their meanings out of this specific context. Through the tools SUPERFLEX investigates communicative processes in which power, hegemony, assertion and oppression, the gain and loss of terrain become evident. Various parties, individuals, or groups enter the scene with strong personal and specific interests. They constantly influence how the tool is constructed and/or used. The set-up structures can be redefined by users, which can finally lead to changes in the tool itself. The resulting scenarios, a constantly changing succession of possibilities and meanings, are then continued as long as the interest

(Figure 0035)

remains alive. . . . All tools share the aspect of empowerment: eg., having their own energy supply … In their tools SUPERFLEX attempts to create conditions for the production of new ways of thinking, acting, speaking and imagining."[2] The final words of the introduction summarize this appeal, "This book is intended as both a fund of information and a tool in its own right. Read and use!"

SUPERFLEX measures its success in terms of offerings that proceed from the artists to the public and return to the artists. Instead of casting an artist's intention in a rigid form, these art works develop independently of the artists' inclinations. They are fulfilled when they are used or adapted by others, not when they are collected or displayed.

It is significant that the group name, SUPERFLEX, is better known than the names of the individual members. Bjørnstjerne Christiansen, Jakob Fenger, and Rasmus Nielsen neither seek individual acclaim nor deserve it. This is because they share the creative role with experts who provide the skills and information they lack, with populations that provide knowledge of local traditions and conditions, and with those who adopt the tools and use them as they choose. Self-organization is SUPERFLEX's term for ground-up decision making and unpredictable results. It allows the power of art to shift from the artist's self-glorification to the public's self-sufficiency.

Guaraná Power (2003 and ongoing) is an art project by SUPERFLEX that takes its name from an energy soft drink that is manufactured by a farmers' cooperative in the Brazilian Amazon. It qualifies as a SUPERFLEX tool because the artists collaborated with the guaraná berry growers to help them gain independence from the controlling power of multinational corporations. The corporations precipitated an economic crisis for the farmers when they drove the price paid for berries down 80 percent over a four-year period. SUPERFLEX and the farmers pooled their resources to escape the corporate monopoly. The farmers contributed agricultural expertise and knowledge of traditional values. SUPERFLEX contributed motivation and the money they raised through the art community. Together they formed an organization that now produces a drink that is distinct from the soft drinks made with guaraná berries by multinational corporations. *Guaraná Power* is a tonic that invigorates consumers who drink it. It also invigorates the producers because the project empowers poor farmers to liberate themselves from the dominance of superpowers. In addition, it invigorates the local ecosystems because, when farmers gain the power to choose their own forms of agriculture, they often reinstall traditional practices.

(Figure 0036)

Superchannel (1999) is an actual company started by SUPERFLEX. It functions as a tool because it enables individual people and communities to produce their own Internet TV programs on their own web channels. At the time of this writing, *Superchannel* had 31 channels and was offering 1,433 shows. This network of local studios provides an alternative to corporate programming. It is television for and by the people. Every show has its own live online chat room where viewers can discuss the program and talk to broadcasters. Because this live Internet TV uses cheap, existing technology and software, it is accessible to anyone with an ordinary computer, a video camera, and an Internet connection. *Superchannel* also welcomes proposals from people who want to start their own channels. The software allows anyone with basic computer know-how to produce and broadcast a show, which is then accessed through the *Superchannel* website. *Superchannel* redistributes power from the top of media command posts to the bottom. It allows human energy to flow in all directions in the manner of dynamic ecosystems.

Supercopy is a concept SUPERLEX developed when it applied the principle of dispersing power to information. The group concluded that intellectual property rights are damaging to both culture and the environment because they limit access to information. Thus SUPERFLEX established *Copyshop* (2005) to support unprotected distribution and information sharing. *Copyshop* provides a place where original texts and images can be photocopied and modified according to the needs and whims of users.

The shop also serves as an information forum where discussions are held to investigate the control and value of information. In this way, *Copyshop* combines the production, the distribution, and the critique of intellectual property. It also sells copyright-busting items like "the world's first open-source beer." Under a Creative Commons license, anyone can alter the ingredients and distribute the beer as long as the new version of the recipe is published and the originators are credited. SUPERFLEX also extended open sharing beyond the limits established by many progressive thinkers when the group expressed its disapproval of property rights that only guard the intellectual products of people in the developed world. They do not protect indigenous peoples in the undeveloped world. SUPERFLEX's objection took the form of acceptance that traditional wisdom exists in the public domain, unprotected and therefore free and accessible.

Supergas (1996–ongoing) is a project designed to solve the problem of energy production in impoverished rural communities around the Equator. SUPERFLEX applied imaginative art-making to the practical problem of satisfying family needs within the biotic constraints of the residents' local habitats. This approach is evident in their description of the biogas project: "One of the overall problems in rural areas is the basic need for firewood and other kinds of energy supply. The need for firewood reflects a more basic problem for the developing countries. This is the inability of modern technology to meet the needs of poor people. The fact that the main energy supply is firewood can be seen as a lack of innovation instead of just a lack of firewood … Devastated farmers in marginalized rural areas cannot be held solely responsible for this situation. Complex modern research is out of reach for them. *Supergas* addresses this problem."[3]

SUPERFLEX noted that despite all their power and all their authority, official agencies had failed to alleviate environmental degradation, human poverty, and the energy needs of populations living in underdeveloped countries. Thus the artists applied flexible thinking to five standard areas of interaction that are identified below. These approaches distinguish their endeavors from pragmatic projects conducted by people who are not artists.

Organization: SUPERFLEX reversed the standard top-down structure of energy production and distribution. Instead of a centrally owned and operated facility, it allocated ownership, management, and output to individual households. The domestically scaled biogas digester they developed offers an inexpensive, nonpolluting, and environment-enhancing source of energy for people who currently live beyond the reach of the electrical grid. These biogas plants run on cattle dung and sunlight and are capable of supplying a family of 10 with enough gas for cooking and illumination.

Economics: SUPERFLEX collaborated with a Tanzanian agricultural organization called Surude (Sustainable Rural Development) to mass-produce the user-friendly biogas unit as a commercial product. SUPERFLEX explains, "One of the important aspects of the project was trying to capitalize it. . . The reason to capitalize it was that we believe that one of the main problems on the African continent is the lack of possibilities for consumers. We wanted to focus on the modern African consumer as a target for investment (and not only aid-invest)."[4] As a tool, Surude not only serves the needs of individual households, it helps stimulate the economies of undeveloped countries.

Psychology: Fenger, Nielsen, and Christiansen initiated the biogas project by traveling to Tanzania to meet with villagers and local officials. Their purpose was "to establish a system that is in tune with actually existing local conditions rather than imposing an untried idea from elsewhere."[5] Their challenge was to win the confidence of the strangers they hoped to help. Flexible thinking led the artists to introduce themselves wearing khaki shorts and light green shirts. Their outfits differentiated them from the three groups familiar to local residents, and distrusted by them: corporate executives who are motivated by self-interest, tourists who are mainly interested in entertainment, and government bureaucrats who are often corrupt.

Social Service: SUPERFLEX rejected the generosity of aid givers because it is not empowering. Indeed, aid often worsens power inequalities by fostering the dependencies of aid recipients. The group explains, "We do not wish to impose a prevailing ideology on people–the families are perfectly

(Figure 0037)

free to choose. Nor is the biogas project a gift. We might compare it to a Western family buying a car."[6]

Marketing: SUPERFLEX considered how to make a strange and alien innovation like a biogas plant desirable to its intended users. Because the plants function like furnaces, oil tanks, septic tanks, and sewage treatment plants, they lack appeal as commercial products. In order to make them more seductive, SUPERFLEX painted them a brilliant orange, emblazoned them with a stylish logo, and encouraged customers to install them conspicuously in the front of their homes in the manner of a luxury item to impress neighbors. Nielsen explains, "We wanted the system to be very visible–so you can follow the production of gas. We like the fact that although these are basically shit containers, there's an aesthetic element. It can be low-scale cheap technology, but it doesn't have to look like shit."[7]

In all these ways, SUPERFLEX channels power from entrepreneurs to consumers, from governments to citizens, and from corporations to workers. These goals converged in the biogas project by empowering geographically remote households to gain control over their own energy production. The units improve the health of the people and their habitats. Erosion decreases as trees root and grow. Food production increases due to the compost materials produced by biogas plants. Water contamination diminishes because human and animal wastes are diverted. These are significant improvements for people who are unambiguous losers in the worldwide competition for technologies and economic security.

But SUPERFLEX tools also act upon the unambiguous winners in the global competition for power. They distribute doses of power to circumvent the bullying tactics of mega corporations, the ineffectiveness of international aid agencies, and the rigidity of government bureaucracies. SUPERFLEX overhauls human power from the tips to the toes of society.

(Figure 0034)   *SUPERFLEX, Guarana Power, 2003, Four color advertisement, Courtesy the artists,*
(Figure 0035)   *SUPERFLEX in collaboration with the University of Tropical Agriculture in Cambodia,*
                 SUPERGAS biogas system, Cambodia, 2001, Courtesy the artists
(Figure 0036)   *SUPERFLEX, Don't Waste Waste, Superflex Tools book, 2002, Courtesy the artists*
(Figure 0037)   *SUPERFLEX, Trapholt SUPERTEENS, SUPERCHANNEL, 2001, Trapholt Museum of Modern Art,*
                 Applied Art, Design and Furniture Design, Denmark, Courtesy the artists
                 Full Color images and supplemental images at www.Avant-Guardians.com

Exploring Power

The following projects estimate the extent of your power in the world.

1. Visualize 10 categories of human relationships. Depict the power you exert upon them and/or the power they exert upon you. Choose five groups of people with whom you personally interact and five groups with whom you do not have personal relationships. Personal acquaintances might include your classmates, your family, your neighbors, and your teammates. Impersonal relationships might include the National Guard, dairy farmers, sneaker manufacturers, medical care providers, and religious leaders. Your representations may be abstract or representational. They may take the form of diagrams, charts, spreadsheets, graphs, or any other manner of representing the distribution of power between you and other humans.

2. Visualize your power within five contexts in which you have been present. For example, you might consider yourself in a garden, bedroom, classroom, mall, airplane, forest, ocean, etc. Depict the power you exert upon them and/or the power they exert upon you. This representation may be abstract or representational. It may take the form of diagrams, charts, spreadsheets, graphs, or any other manner of representing the distribution of power between you and your environment.

3. SUPERFLEX measures a person's power according to his or her independence from corporate and government influence. It equates power with self-sufficiency. By this measure, few people living in advanced technological societies are powerful. The vast majority are completely dependent upon a remote network of humans and technologies to provide the commodities and perform the services that sustain them. Are you among them?

   If the five statements that follow don't apply to you, discuss why they are false. If they do apply to you, identify the behavioral changes that you would have to undergo in order to make them false. How would these changes affect your power?

   Currently my life support depends on electricity.

   Currently my life support depends on mechanized transit.

   Currently my life support depends on industrial processes.

   Currently my life support depends on money.

4. This self-empowering art project will be performed in class. It is designed to help release you from some prevailing form of dependency. Choose one activity from the following list, or select one of your own. Perform it without relying on manufactured or purchased materials:

> Decorate your body
> Tell time
> Forecast weather
> Gather water
> Create light
> Groom yourself
> Stay warm/dry
> Communicate over distances
> Record information
> Be entertained

5. SUPERFLEX exemplifies the principle of catalyzing change through cooperation, not force. Their mandate to cooperate applies to humans and to ecosystems. The following project is designed to foster ecosystem cooperation. Your creative partners are four basic environmental forces: hot, cold, wet, dry. These forces have been selected because, since prehistory, they have stimulated the human impulse to exert power by controlling environments.

   Create a work of art in which you engage hot, cold, wet, or dry. Please allow this sensory partner to determine the medium, the process, and the theme of your work. There are two ways to complete this exploration. Either the forces of hot, cold, wet, or dry will produce a permanent physical change, such as shrinking or staining, or they will be the cause of a temporary change, such as a sound, movement, or smell. As a result, your work of art may be static (an object) or kinetic (a moving object or a performance).

6. The following report demonstrates the dilemmas involved with directing human power even when the intention is to use this power for responsible stewardship of the Earth.

   Thai elephants were classified as animals with a high risk of extinction by the International Union for the Conservation of Nature in 1988. By then, their numbers had dwindled because their forest habitats had decreased precipitously. In 1990 forest supporters succeeded in banning logging. This threw domesticated elephants out of work. Elephant unemployment plunged their owners into poverty. This caused more declines in elephant populations, because their owners became too poor to provide the 400 pounds of food required to sustain a 6,000-pound elephant each day. At the present time elephants are dying, their owners are impoverished, but forests are returning.

   Establish your position within this controversy and outline a project that activates your position. Consider selecting one of SUPERFLEX's strategies: organization, economics, psychology, marketing, and social services.

7. Like SUPERFLEX, Matthew Barney (1967–) has concocted a tool kit, but his kit develops his physical and mental capacities and thereby maximizes his personal powers. Barney strives to amass, command, and apply significant quantities of the Earth's material and energetic resources to his art practice. Early in his career, Barney applied boundary-defying aspirations to his own body by conducting, recording, and displaying physical workouts. The series *Drawing Restraint* (1989–1993) documents such extraordinary physical feats as walking across a ceiling. It also documents Barney's exceptional efforts to retain his precious energies. In one case the artist attempted to avoid depleting his bodily power by actually attaching prosthetic devices that sealed all of his body orifices. Throughout his career, Barney has continually escalated obstacles as a means to reach new plateaus of accomplishment and exceed former capabilities. Most recently he has manifested his powers by creating a series of film epics. Each seems to surpass his former achievement of extravagance, ambition, and mastery.

    SUPERFLEX and Barney both strive to augment power. However, Barney amasses power, while SUPERFLEX disperses power. Please explore the possibility that these approaches may be interdependent, like breathing in (accumulating power) in order to breathe out (expending power), or bending your knees (accumulating power) to make it possible to leap (expending power). Create a work of art that expresses the theme of power metaphorically, either as an accumulation like Barney, a distribution like SUPERFLEX, or as a merger of the two.

(1) SUPERFLEX, e-mail statement, January 18, 2006. superflux.mailing@gmail.com.
(2) The Editors, SUPERFLEX, SUPERFLEX /Tools Book. Germany: Verlag der Buchhandlung Walther Konig, 2003. http://www.SUPERFLEX.net/text/publications/toolsintro.shtml
(3) SUPERFLEX/Tools/Environment. http://www.SUPERFLEX.net/tools/supergas/invitation.shtml
(4) SUPERFLEX, e-mail correspondence with the author. November 2004.
(5) Åsa Nacking, Afterall 1998, Issue 0. http://www.SUPERFLEX.net/text/articles/an_exchange_between. shtml
(6) Ibid.
(7) Glenn Sumi, SUPERFLEX. NOW, Vol. 24 No. 4. September 2329, 2004. http://www.nowtoronto.com/is-sues/2004-09-23/cover_story.php

Nature

"Nature" is a key word in the vocabulary of most English-speaking people, but it is suspiciously absent from the discourse conducted by professional ecologists. The word is often disqualified from the rigorous scientific discipline of ecology because it is replete with metaphoric associations and imbued with emotional reverberations. Its persistent use within popular usage, however, reveals historic attitudes about the nonhuman realm that linger into the current era. These attitudes are reinforced each time we use common phrases that include the word "nature." "Going back to nature" indicates a return to some simple, more primitive state of existence. "An impulse of nature" is a stimulus that evades conscious control. "Letting nature take its course" is a euphemism for abandoning efforts to control a situation. "In the nature of the beast" refers to some inherent quality that is unaffected by training or education. "A call to nature" is a polite term for the need for a toilet, a function that is commonly isolated as an unsocial activity. The most poignant expression has been reserved for last. "Human nature" designates the qualities that have escaped the dictates of socialization. In each of these instances, the word "nature" suggests that life is more authentic in the absence of human will and manipulation. This connotation is confirmed by the following synonyms for the word "unnatural:" artificial, designed, and civilized.

Nature: An Ecocentric Interpretation

Where can one find this virginal state of nature? Since the dawn of history, hominids affected the surrounding material world by altering it to achieve comfort, security, and convenience. For instance, they escaped the vagaries of season and weather by wrapping themselves in animal skins, building fires, and occupying caves. Such efforts to improve the quality of life by controlling environmental conditions became magnified when humans began to disperse, taking up residence in searing deserts and frigid tundra. Schemes for altering the environment have evolved from fur wraps to climate-controlled hundred-story skyscrapers. Our markings and manipulations are evident throughout the globe. We routinely shape our environment by penetrating mountains to lay roads, damming rivers to generate nuclear energy, boring rock to extract underground resources, and so forth. All of these manipulations enable our species to prevail in the competition to survive and multiply. From this powerful advantage, infatuation with images of virginal nature may prove to be as fatal as blatant control.

Historically, the cultures that succeed have been the most skilled at commandeering resources and extorting energies from nature's bounty. Unfortunately, actions designed to augment comfort, convenience, and security can backfire. Run-offs, seepages, sludge, and toxins are just a few of the unintended and undesired consequences of these pursuits. Our zeal to triumph over nature could make us grand slam champions in the winner-takes-all contest that obliterates our own species. We may literally "make a killing:" our own.

Dave Burns and Matias Viegener are attempting to sever the linguistic association of the word 'nature' with a realm that is untouched by humans and therefore unspoiled. The artists have introduced a metaphor that offers a more accurate indicator of the extent of humanity's intrusions upon the Earth.

(Figure 0038)

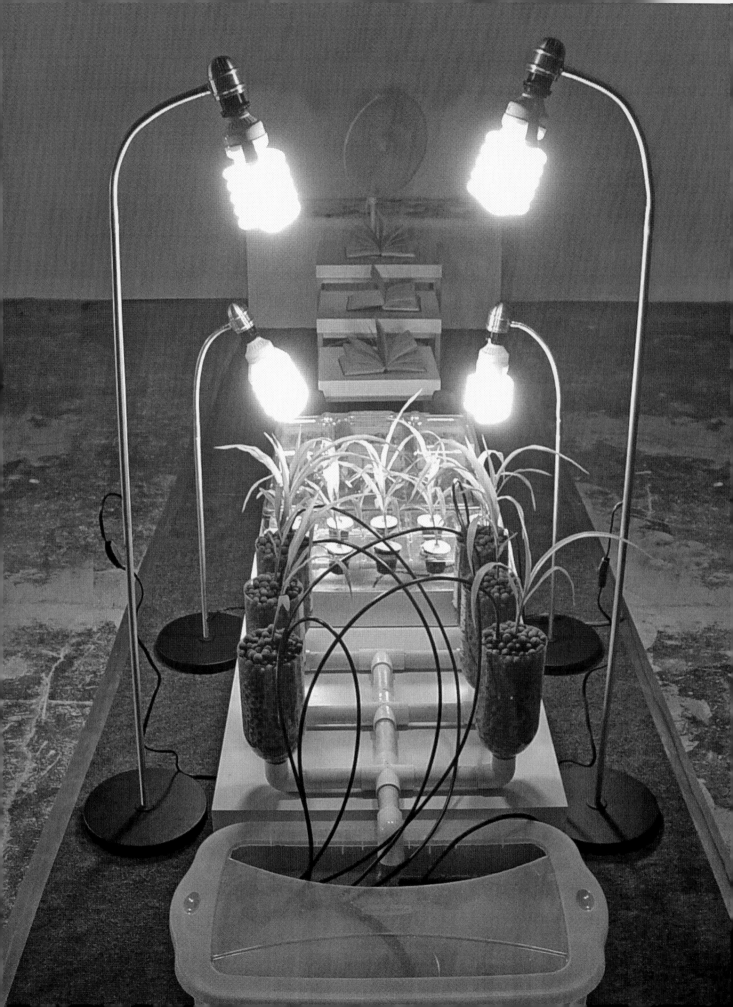

Dave Burns

Born 1970 Santa Monica, California
1993 Cal Arts School of Fine Arts, BFA photography
2005 University of California, Irvine, MFA studio arts

Matias Viegener

Born 1959 Buenos Aires, Argentina
Columbia University, BA
University of California, Los Angeles, MA and Ph.D. comparative literature

What single plant could serve as a symbol of the contemporary state of 'nature'? Would you select a mighty oak, a delicate lily, or a hardy dandelion? Should wild strawberries be chosen to envision nature's bountiful offerings, or eucalyptus to signal its vitality, or poison ivy to indicate its dangers?

Dave Burns and Matias Viegener sought a plant to cast in their allegory of the human ability to regulate, subjugate, and manipulate the environment. "We chose to work with corn because corn is so pervasive in the food chain in our culture. It comprises the majority of the carbs we eat. It is a sugar substitute, a feed for livestock, a source of oil and cereal. It is a hidden ingredient in most processed foods. Corn holds a mythic place as a sacred new-world grain, source of sugar, fiber, ethanol, animal fodder, popcorn, alcohol, plastic polymers, synthesized building materials and now, through genetic manipulation, custom pharmaceuticals. Ancient cultures used corn for fuel, shelter, fabric, symbolic figurines, and food that would survive long winters. The corn plant is by legend the essential gift of the Native Americans to the European colonizers, who would never have survived the bitter New England winters without it. Thus, corn has a central place at the Thanksgiving table. Everyone is fond of corn."[1]

Corn's puny form 7,000 years ago testifies to the commanding powers of human management. It was then that native peoples living in Mexico domesticated corn. Ancient cobs were less than two inches long. There was only one cob per plant, only one or two rows of kernels on each cob, and only a few small kernels in each row. Ancient kernels had hard casings that made them difficult to eat. In order to make corn more productive, sweet, and mouth-watering, we humans subjected corn to two kinds of management. We either manipulated germ plasma before conception through hybridization and selection, or we controlled the environment after conception through pesticides and fertilizers. These techniques allowed us to concoct high-yield 'supercorn' which, despite many improvements, lacked the two advantages of ancient corn. Supercorn was not resistant to drought and pests. Monsanto and other giants of industry discovered a new form of manipulation to bolster the defenses of designer corn–genetic modification (GM). Such corporate sponsors acclaim GM as a boon to feed a hungry world. Many concerned citizens believe it could be a danger with unknown consequences.

(Figure 0039)

Burns and Viegener created a humorous allegory with a clinical veneer. *Corn Study* (2004) asserts the need for corn to resist its manipulation by humans, who, after centuries of tampering, are now intruding directly upon its genetics. The artists might have dramatized this theme by enlisting the corn into a freedom-fighter brigade. Such a metaphor would affirm corn's powers of self-defense. Instead, they summoned the forces of education, not revolt, and thereby created an allegory for corn's need for instruction. Burns and Viegener sent corn to school to learn the grizzly details of its history. They reversed William Wordsworth's famous quote, "Let Nature be your teacher,"[2] by assigning nature student status. The artists explain, "We are changing the context in which corn is raised. We are going to the source by treating seeds like foster kids, like Head Start. We believe it is possible to change the environment by changing thought. It is not necessary to use physical alterations."

To fulfill this mission, the artists established the world's first academy for corn. The academy supports open admissions, assigns no grades, and charges no tuition. Still, it has a complete curriculum, a schedule of classes, and recommended course loads. "Our project is a response to the escalating manipulation of the corn plant and the desire to develop a new relationship with the biosphere. While great effort has been put into the human understanding of plants, their culture, and their genetic structure, very little has been expended to educate the corn and teach it about humans who control its fate. When we considered teaching the corn the history of its own species, we recognized this as folly, since the corn already knows itself, as well as possessing an innate knowledge of botany, ecology, chemistry, and physics. In the future our curriculum may also address astrophysics to prepare for the eventuality of our species' exodus from the planet that we seem intent upon ruining. Corn in some future form will no doubt accompany us to the stars."

The artists' parody of the manipulated state of 'nature' and its need to bolster its defenses against human incursions takes the form of an accelerated learning program. The school is set up on 10 tabletops with different learning stations. A narrow pathway functions as the school's central hallway. As visitors walk down this path between two rows of metal tables, they encounter corn students and classrooms, laboratories, and textbooks. As in most educational institutions, the advancement of the corn students correlates with their ages. Their progress from seed to maturity occurs in stages in carefully controlled hydroponics systems. By including this synthetic growth environment, the installation reinforces the 'unnatural' conditions of a 'natural' process. Hydroponics replaces old-fashioned water with a chemical solution; it substitutes traditional dirt with growth medium; it exchanges sunshine for grow lamps; and it delivers air by electric fans.

The vats of bubbling hydroponics solution greet visitors when they enter the installation. The health of these plants manifests the success of these manipulations. Visitors then walk through the tallest corn plants and past the plastic domes of seedlings growing in an artificial medium. The lowest bin in the installation contains nine wooden boxes of mixed corn seeds. Some of the seeds are genetically modified. The artists explain, "We included all the cultivars and variants we could find, even genetically modified ones, because GM seeds still belong to the species. We recognize that all species are always being modified, either artificially or naturally. They are all deserving of respect and education. In that sense we're critical of the strict naturalists who see all manipulation as evil. The philosophy was to educate the species, to generate consciousness. In this sense our view of nature is very inclusive—we include ourselves as well, since everything human also evolved from nature. The distinction we do seek to make is between wisdom and folly, which is a cultural and ethical category. We want to catalyze a movement in all species, in all of nature, toward wisdom and insight. The key to this understanding is to be attentive to the nonhuman world."[3]

As the path proceeds beyond the seed bins, the tables become progressively taller. They display stacks of books used in the corn's extensive curriculum, which includes philosophy, literature, the Bible, poetry, classics of Western civilization, current events, the history of colonialism, etc. The top book in each stack is open. Two oscillating fans rustle the pages; their breeze sweeps down to the corn itself. The artists say the fans are there to "blow the knowledge through the pages on to the corn seeds, like pollen drifting through the air."

Another barrage of information spews from speakers that function as subliminal audio-delivery systems. One channel presents tapes of emotive material oriented to the right brain. It offers the seedlings inspiring material about hope, growth, and good relationships as encapsulated in the optimistic pop music of the 1960s and 70s: "I'd Like to Teach the World to Sing," "Let the Sun Shine In," and "Joy to the World." Concurrently, a second channel delivers intellectual left-brain instruction; it broadcasts archival tapes by Theodore Roosevelt, Malcolm X., Gloria Steinem, Noam Chomsky, Albert Einstein, Martin Luther King, Al Sharpton, and so forth. Then students encounter instructional tapes. Some offer cultural studies, language, history, mythology, economics, socialism, psychology, and philosophy, while others offer self-help on how to reduce anxiety, get centered, and find your true self. The installation culminates at a table heaped with brochures and pamphlets on subjects that range from hydroponics to space colonization.

Corn Study makes double use of the force of education as a metaphor. At the same time that it instructs corn about its subjugation to humans, it instructs humans about the fallacy of believing that nature is untainted or that nature's wisdom exceeds human faculties. Corny parody was adopted to accomplish human instruction: "We want to pose questions in a way that doesn't automatically turn the public off. The way in which our populism is manifested is love of corniness. Corniness is a way of communicating a meaning that won't be heard in any other way."

The artists report that *Corn Study* was doubly successful. One success was hoped for: "We created a world. We added a community. People responded." The other success was unanticipated: "Before the exhibition, we grew some corn outdoors and observed its growth. When we repeated the process in the school, the corn grew twice as fast and twice as happily. This is not a scientific claim, but something happened. The plants were greener, meatier, and healthier." The results suggest that corn prospers when it is placed in an environment that nurtures, instead of exploits, its potential.

This installation conveys the artists' belief that nature needs to learn how to fortify itself and humans need to learn how to fortify nature. "Today's methods of growing corn have dreadful consequences for the environment. Our natural resources are being plundered at an accelerated rate, with diminishing genetic diversity driving new extinctions and permanently altering our ecosystem. Maybe corn can resist contributing to this degradation." In a written statement they concluded, "While it may take many generations before the outcome of our experiment can be demonstrated, we are hoping for positive mutations and raised consciousness in the corn, to be passed along to other species. At this stage of global development, humans can no longer be entrusted with full stewardship of the environment. Perhaps if other species can intervene, they will do a better job."[4]

On the closing day of the exhibition, Burns and Viegener conducted a ritual meal that summoned nostalgic notions of 'nature' as a rural haven and juxtaposed it with high-tech operations of engineering and manufacture. The artists served a contemporary corn harvest: cornbread, corn dogs, popcorn, corn chips, cornflakes, corn syrups, corn grits, but they were like country boys in jeans, plaid shirts, and straw hats. They hoped that those who shared the meal might join them in offering thanks to the corn, a potent symbol of the extent to which the nonhuman environment has been reconfigured to serve civilization.

(Figure 0038)   *Dave Burns and Matias Viegener, Corn Study, detail, 2004, Mixed media, Dimensions variable, Courtesy the artists, Photography Austin Young*

(Figure 0039)   *Dave Burns and Matias Viegener, Corn Study, detail, 2004, Mixed media, Dimensions variable, Courtesy the artists, Photography Austin Young*

Full Color images and supplemental images at www.Avant-Guardians.com

Exploring Nature

1. Have you ever experienced virginal nature? This question applies to the inhabitants of the 21st century. But it could also have been asked millions of years ago, and then too it would have been difficult to answer. This is because, before life began, nature consisted of chemistry and physics. Nothing existed but stone, air, water, and energy. Then biology was added to the mix. Even the first single-celled organisms changed the complexion of nature. Human beings are a continuation of this evolution. The belief that nature provides a functional and aesthetic model persists, when in actuality natural conditions perpetually change, even in the absence of human influence.

2. The same people who seek surviving evidence of nature's majesty on vacations often contribute to its ruin at work. Francis Bacon, an esteemed Renaissance philospher, can't be blamed for this state of affairs. Five hundred years ago he proclaimed, "We cannot command nature except by obeying her." Bacon's recommendation to command nature became installed as a credo of progress. However, his urging to proceed through obedience has been largely ignored. Burns and Viegener apply this unsettling discrepancy to corn. Diller + Scofidio and John Roloff choose water, and Alan Sonfist chooses soil, to address this theme.

Diller + Scofidio and John Roloff created *Pure Mix*. The title of the work reveals the contradiction between 'purity' and 'mixtures' that seems to pervade human relationships with nature. On the one hand we relish unspoiled wilderness, beaches, and deserts. On the other hand we continually tamper with them. The artists addressed this discrepancy in the winter of 2004 when they were invited to use water to create an outdoor work of art for The Snow Show near the Baltic Sea. *Pure Mix* is a 1,000-square-foot, frozen water mosaic. It was constructed by removing harbor ice and filling the rectangular cavities with 170 liters of water the artists imported from around the globe. Each of the 81 ice blocks was carefully etched with a brand name, logo, or geographical location to identify the source of the specialty water. There were designer waters that had been processed and packaged by Perrier, Volvic, Vittel, and Gucci. There was also Iranian water, Catholic holy water, water from the River Jordan, etc. This frozen spreadsheet presented the political, religious, and commercial roles water plays in human lives. It also provided evidence of our schizophrenic relationship with water. We degrade it, but we also undertake elaborate efforts to purify it. We squander it, and then we pay dearly to purchase it. We pollute it, and then we clean ourselves with it. The work continued after the spring thaw, when these culturally significant water samples trickled into the open sea, but no one can say how long they will remain there before being recaptured or altered by human interventions.

Alan Sonfist does not believe that once virginity in nature is lost, it is gone forever. Since the 1970s he has dedicated his art practice to the resilience of nature to reestablish its virginal conditions even after they have become tainted. In fact, Sonfist uses the term 'virgin' to describe the condition of purity in nature that he aspires to recapture. Sonfist described *Seed Catcher* as "a pool of virgin earth to collect the seeds of nearby forests through wind and animal migration."[5] The piece was conceived in 1973 and realized in 1975 as *Pool of Earth* in Lewiston, New York. It consists of a 6-foot-deep hole, 25 feet in diameter that was dug in the midst of Love Canal, an area that William T. Love envisioned at the end of the 19th century as a dream community. This dream did not come true. The city of Niagara Falls used the undeveloped area as a disposal site for waste from the petrochemical industry. Later, the United States Army buried waste from experiments in chemical warfare there. After that, it became the dumping ground for the toxic waste from private chemical and plastics manufacturers. Acres of contaminated wasteland surround the circular cavity that Sonfist created. He filled it with fresh, healthy earth and then left it alone. Over time, the seeds that fell upon this little patch of wholesome soil sprouted. Birds and insects returned. *Pool of Earth* continues to thrive. It is an inspiring symbol of the vigor of the life force.

A. All the artists in this chapter address the fickle quality of human interactions with nature. Their works demonstrate that nature is something we mess up, fix up, ignore, engineer, admire, exploit, replenish, worship, etc. Their works apply this theme to a plant, to water, and to soil. Create a work of art that demonstrates contradictory human behaviors that apply to an animal.

B. Burns and Viegener confront the following contradictions:

They protest human interventions by intervening.

They oppose human control by controlling.

They contest human manipulation by manipulating.

Compare their strategies with those employed by Alan Sonfist and Diller + Scofidio and John Roloff who also challenge human intervention, control, and manipulation.

3. The following questions pose some of the crucial quandaries of the contemporary era:

Can we retain high crop yield and avoid contaminating soil, food, and water with pesticides, fertilizers, hormones, etc.?

Can we continue to enjoy the mobility provided by modern forms of transportation and eliminate toxic emissions?

Can we participate in the convenience and pleasures offered by commodities, and refrain from cluttering our minds with the tasks associated with mining or harvesting, transporting, manufacturing, transporting, storing, transporting, selling, transporting, using, transporting, and discarding?

Select one of the environmental challenges listed above, or any other. Create a collaborative work of art in which you and your partner represent opposing points of view. For instance, you may choose to be an optimist, while your partner presents the position of a realist, pessimist, skeptic, or fatalist.

4. Dictionary definitions of the word "nature" can be summarized as follows: "Nature" encompasses the material world surrounding humanity, and exists independently of human activities. This means "nature" includes plants, rocks, all the earth's features, all of its forces and processes, the weather, sea, mountains. Accordingly, "nature" excludes people, culture, and the effects of culture on the land, such as suburbs, cities, roads, mines, oilfields, cell towers, farms, airports, and malls. The following excerpt from a news story epitomizes this separation:

    "Welcome to the camp experience in the age of the mosquito. For the first time in at least a decade when the skies were clear, the 92nd Street Y camp's fabled overnight event under the stars would take place indoors, in Manhattan instead of at the Henry Kaufmann Campground in Pearl River, N.Y. Instead of a campfire, there would be a circle of flashlights. The s'mores would be made with Marshmallow Fluff. Officials at the Y said that out of concern for the safety of the children and parents' fears about the West Nile virus, they did not want campers exposed to mosquitoes during the active feeding hours at night."[6]

    Synthetic experiences that replace nature prevail throughout contemporary culture. Create a work of art that provides one example of this phenomenon.

5. Unless artists claim the entire material world as their art works, they have no choice but to select an object or a concept to represent nature in its entirety. Corn, water, and dirt serve this purpose in the examples noted above. Select an example, metaphor, or symbol that expresses your view of the state of nature and manifest it in an art work.

6. Nature consists of objects (living and nonliving) and forces (sedimentation, accretion, oxidation, gravity, wind, etc). Select one object or one force as your theme. Present it in three different ways:

    A. Depict it.

    B. Interpret it.

    C. Manipulate it.

    For example, if you chose wind as your theme, you might depict it by rendering whirling leaves, you might interpret it by imagining the wind whispering in your ear; you might manipulate it by capturing hot air in a balloon.

(1) Unless otherwise noted, all quotes from an interview with the artists, April 4, 2005

(2) William Wordsworth The Tables Turned, 1798

(3) Correspondence with Matias Viegener, January 3, 2006

(4) Matias Viegener and Dave Burns, Corn Study. http://fritzhaeg.com/garden/initiatives/gardenlabshow/participants/viegenerburns_text.html

(5) Conversation with the author in January 2006.

(6) Gootman, Elissa "Camping In, and Leaving the Bugs Out". New York Times, Saturday, July 15, 2000, Page A1.

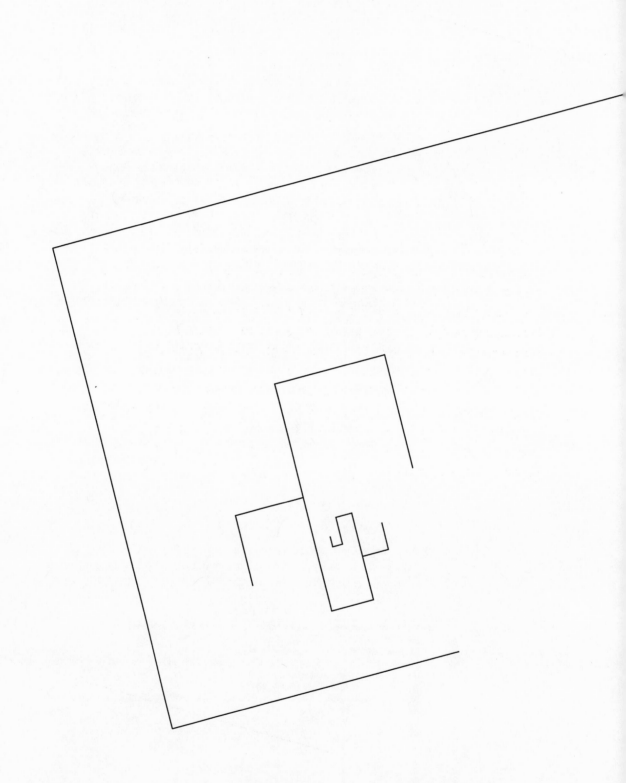

Globalism

When the first space probe traveled far enough from the Earth to capture the entire planet in the viewfinder of its cameras, the picture created a powerful symbol of global unification. Suddenly it was possible for humans to envision the whole globe existing within the range of individual opportunity, access, and experience. This emblematic image inspired a surge of hope for worldwide peace and prosperity. Believers demoted the significance of national loyalties, border patrols, and protective tariffs in order to promote the notion of free international passage for people, capital, information, and technology. This cozy image of a global village evokes globe-trotting world citizens behaving like neighbors. Globalism melds "the ends of the earth" and its "four corners" into a unified sphere.

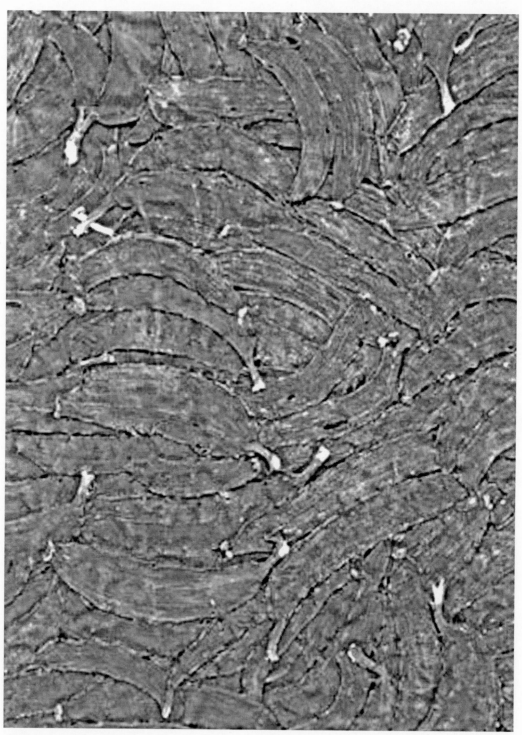

(Figure 0040)

Globalism: An Ecocentric Interpretation

The Gaia hypothesis,[1] which is favored by many environmentalists, supports a cohesive view. It depicts Earth as an elaborate, synchronized, self-regulating feedback mechanism and asserts that all species of organisms share one resource base. But that is not where the Gaia hypothesis ends. It also posits that global conditions are the summation of small-scale behaviors within microhabitats. For this reason, many environmentalists support such locally scaled endeavors as local currencies, community gardens, neighborhood recycling facilities, district-based material exchanges, and regional trading partners. All these initiatives involve direct engagement with indigenous conditions and materials.

By dominating contemporary world views, globalism often thrusts localism into a defensive posture. Global superhighways, whether they are paved or electronic, offer excitement and adventure. In comparison, local trails near home often seem pallid and provincial. Would you rather board a bus, subway, automobile, train, ship, or jet? All these means of transport consume energy and deplete resources. Furthermore, they all have local and global effects. But their effects are hardly equal.

Shelley Sacks bucks the globalism trend. Her skepticism is based on her observation that global peace and prosperity are enjoyed by few at the expense of many. Global exchange does not guarantee equitable distribution. Sacks notes that globalism actually provides an opportunity for businesses to circumvent local interests in order to leverage the labor and resources of underdeveloped regions. Her solution is to create more locally scaled economies that bypass the World Trade Organization, International Monetary Fund, and World Bank.

(Figure 0041)

Shelley Sacks

Born 1950 Bloemfontein, South Africa
1972 University of Cape Town, diploma, fine art
1972 University of Cape Town, postgraduate advanced diploma, fine art
1974–1975 Akademie fur Bildende Kunst, Hamburg, postgraduate study
1973 –1975, 1977, 1980 Free International University, Germany
1985 Cape Town, Interdisciplinary African Studies, MA program

"Forty years and more we've sung the banana song
In gratitude to Life. In gratitude to You
Who buy the fruit we grow
From the earth, under the sky.

Then comes 'free trade' like the tropical hurricane
Battering us, knocking down our protection;
Exposing our vulnerability.
Multinational companies and United States politics
Conspire to destroy our lives
On the hilltops, on the hillsides, and in the valleys.
We see our lives shriveling like dried banana skins,
Savaged and discarded by those who proclaim: 'In God We Trust'
More destructive than the raging hurricane."[2]

This heartfelt lament evokes the life experience of its author, Fremont Lawrence, head of social affairs for the St. Lucia Banana Growers Association. Its bitter sentiments are embodied in an art work by Shelley Sacks entitled *Exchange Values: Images of Invisible Lives* (1996 – ongoing). In this installation, the enigmatic allure of stretched sheets of dried and blackened banana skins beckons viewers to pause and seek their significance. Sacks obsessively collected, meticulously dried, and laboriously stitched the skins from bananas she had purchased in a market near her home in the United Kingdom. She then labeled each sheet with the number stamped on the crate in which the bananas had been transported. These numbers allowed her to trace the fruit back to its place of origin and the specific farmers who cultivated it. Sacks then undertook an arduous journey, through the rugged terrain of the tropical rainforests of St. Lucia in the Caribbean's Windward Islands, to meet the farmers. She returned with the recorded voices of farmers giving personal accounts of their working and living conditions. A recording was attached to each sheet of banana skin in the installation.

While the sweet smell of bananas calls to mind the familiar pleasures of a comfort food, the taut appearance of these sheets evokes anguish. This aesthetic contrast dramatizes the economic disparity between consumers and producers participating in the banana market. Memories of eating pleasures are thereby linked to the farmers' indignation and despair over their victimization by the worldwide banana market.

For example, the crate number R610145 identifies Andre Rigobert's farm. Sacks invited Rigobert to track the tangled, competitive course his bananas take, and its effect upon his workers and their families. Forty people depend on the production of bananas from his 10-acre plot. Rigobert reports, "We are left in limbo between Europeans and Americans. We are not isolated in this world, and our culture has been interrelated with cultures of other parts of the world. It is a connection between producers. We are producing bananas in St. Lucia with tools and equipment that were produced in England…. We would like equal treatment–that when we send the bananas to England they will be received in the same way that we received their tools." He then makes a heartfelt appeal to consumers to consider the human and environmental consequences of this transaction. "We watch plants grow. We deal with life. When you buy a pound of our bananas, you are helping small families as against when you buy a Chiquita banana. Then you are just helping a rich international get richer."[3]

Sacks could easily have fulfilled the subtitle of the work by creating "images of invisible lives" with a camera. But instead of exhibiting photographs for viewers to observe, she invites visitors to imagine the growers and thereby internalize their frustrations and insecurities. Individual voices reporting the unsettling details of their lives shatter the anonymity of global economic distribution. Sacks explains her strategy by stating, "Although the consumer listening to the voice of the invisible producer is not, in that moment, involved in changing the status quo in any concrete way, responses suggest that the experience of absence is so tangible–of a producer whose 'skin' is stretched before us, whose voice is inside us– that it stirs one imaginatively, provoking an inward movement that we carry outwards into the world."[4]

The bananas in our fruit bowls don't seem exotic, even though many were grown 3,000 miles away. Most of us take for granted that bananas will appear on market shelves at cheap prices every season o f the year. Nonetheless, with each banana purchase, we are also buying into complex networks of human relationships. Our act affects supermarket employees, truckers, loaders, box manufacturers, cargo ships, farmers, bankers, accountants, bureaucrats, stock market traders, members of the WTO and the IMF. The price we pay reflects interest rates, tariffs, subsidies, tax rates, currency values, commissions, accountings, and advertising.[5] It has been estimated that 50,000 people, representing innumerable global corporations and government agencies, participate in the processes that intervene between

(Figure 0042)

the planting of a seed and the eating of a fruit.[6] This elaborate network of relationships comprises the exchanges between one source of production and one marketplace. It is multiplied by all other competitors in the global marketplace. *Exchange Values* evokes accountings of three competing interests:

International traders seeking market advantage.

Local producers seeking fair wages and safe working conditions.

Consumers seeking cheap prices.

Sacks explains, "We all need money to buy things, and so we usually look for the cheapest things, the best value for our money. On the other hand the producers try to earn as much as possible by looking for ways to maximize their profits. Sometimes this means making things grow bigger and faster, sometimes it means selling things more cheaply to compete with others selling the same things. Now and then the producers are in control of their buying and selling, but in most cases it is big companies who control the workers and the speed of production. Although we all produce things for each other, we have no contact with each other. Being a producer or a consumer in contemporary society means being part of a very complex global economy in which only some participants profit."[7]

Exchange Values personalizes these abstract concepts. Rigobert represents the small-scale, low-tech, individually owned banana farms in the Windward Islands that are forced to compete with large-scale, high-tech corporate banana plantations in Latin America. Although only a few farmers' stories are heard in this installation, thousands share their plight. Sacks suggests the scale of the misfortune by including another 10,000 dried banana skins. They are heaped on the floor encircled by the stretched skins and taped voices.

Windward farmers received decent compensation for their labors as long as the United Kingdom provided protected status to this former colony by guaranteeing tariff-free entry to the European market. However, the establishment of the single European Union market in 1993 required equalization of European import regulations. Intense lobbying and some trade-offs resulted in an agreement that both respected the EU's commitment to the Caribbean and assured liberalization of the market. The narrative might have ended happily for the Windward growers if negotiations had not spread to another continent. Giant U.S. banana multinationals that control Latin America's exports protested. They successfully brought their challenge before the World Trade Organization. By 2006 at the latest, the EU is required to change to a tariff-only system that could be devastating for the small farmers in the Windward Islands.[8] The inability of Caribbean farmers to compete with South American growers is evident when the bananas served to tourists aboard cruise ships docked at St. Lucia bear a Venezuela label![9]

Latin American plantation bananas grow bigger, faster, prettier, and more predictably than those of the Windward Islands. They are referred to as "dollar" bananas because they are also cheaper. Survival of the small farmers who wish to continue growing bananas seems to depend upon adopting one of two contrasting strategies. One is to compete with the immense plantations owned by multinationals by emulating their agricultural practices. This would require a radical shift for the Caribbean growers. Huge monoculture agricultural practices rely upon heavy doses of fertilizers and herbicides to maintain yields and keep diseases at bay. Such methods produce unblemished fruit. In contrast, most Caribbean banana crops are grown with more sustainable techniques. They yield sweeter fruit with marked skins. Referring to the St. Lucia farmers she met, Sacks comments, "Several describe the different ways in which the government compels them to use dreadful chemicals that destroy the land and rivers. They say that these directives from government are a response to the pressures exerted by the U.S.-owned 'dollar' bananas... the huge, straight, blemish-free, highly chemicalized bananas."[10]

The second strategy available to Windward farmers is to base their campaign on fair trade marketing strategies. Under these agreements, certified fair trade farmers receive higher prices than conventional farmers, as long as they conform to superior humanitarian and environmental standards. This approach can only succeed if consumers are willing to support protective policies by paying higher prices. Sacks asks, "When consumers have money in their pockets, is their only responsibility to themselves? Should they seek to buy the cheapest banana? Or should they, having informed themselves as far as possible about the social and environmental costs, consider other criteria in addition to that of cost?"[11]

Sacks is founder of the Social Sculpture Research Unit at Oxford Brookes University. The unit defines "social sculpture" as an interdisciplinary art practice that involves the audience in shaping social processes. Since thought and discussion are its core materials, it recognizes that all humans are artists capable of shaping a democratic, sustainable world.[12] Thus, instead of attempting to reform international institutions that function on a global scale, *Exchange Values* activates individual consumers to make independent purchasing decisions wherever they may be.

(Figure 0040)   *Shelley Sacks in collaboration with banana growers of the Windward Islands, Exchange Values, Sheet of cured banana skin number T330085, 1996-ongoing, Courtesy Shelley Sacks*

(Figure 0041)   *Shelley Sacks in collaboration with banana growers of the Windward Islands, Exchange Values, Nottingham, NOW Festival, Voice of Vitas Emanuelle, 1996 – ongoing, Banana skin 23¾ x 29¾ inches, metal frame 40 x 60 inches, Courtesy Shelley Sacks*

(Figure 0042)   *Shelley Sacks in collaboration with banana growers of the Windward Islands, Exchange Values, The Arena, Oxford, Installation view with participants, 1998, Courtesy Shelley Sacks*

Full Color images and supplemental images at www.Avant-Guardians.com

Exploring Globalism

The world that is referred to in the phrase "the art world" does not only consist of the social, cultural, and economic activities conducted by museums, galleries, and the art press. It also refers to art's many ways of framing global themes. Three approaches to globalism are represented by Shelley Sacks, Marko Pogacnik, and Gu Wenda.

As we have seen, Shelley Sacks provides one example by addressing global exchange networks. This version of globalism gained impetus after the Cold War, when bipolar antagonisms dissolved, opening the doors for goods and information to flow freely across the globe. Electronic technologies accelerated passages through these transnational pathways. Both cultural and physical borders opened for exchange. Unfortunately, information and goods bypass some individuals, while depletions and contaminations beset some ecosystems. Sacks directs the persuasive powers of art to lobby on behalf of the losers in exchanges involving international commerce and production.

Marko Pogacnik (1944–) provides an example of the Gaia approach to globalism by tracing the biological, geological, chemical, and hydrological processes that account for the Earth's resemblance to a single self-regulating organism. A controversial aspect of the hypothesis is the supposition that Earth is a living entity which should be studied in terms of physiology: the oceans and rivers are Earth's blood, the atmosphere is Earth's lungs, the land is Earth's bones, and the living organisms are Earth's senses. Pogacnik believes that this living body is currently suffering from the ill effects of irrigating, damming, developing, and mining. He turned to the medical profession to learn about therapeutic procedures. Instead of surgery and pharmaceuticals, he adopted the ancient healing practice of acupuncture. Pogacnik calls his process "lithopuncture," because the prefix "litho" refers to the mantle of the earth. Just as acupuncturists position needles, Pogacnik carefully locates the pillar-shaped sculptures he creates on sites where he perceives blocked meridians of energy. He explains, "Like the human body, the Earth is a living organism with energy centers and interconnecting veins of energy which one can understand as acupuncture meridians. By touching permanently the acupuncture points of a landscape through stone pillars, it should be possible to get some positive and healing effects upon the respective land."[13]

Gu Wenda (1955–) evokes the unity of human experience and global harmony in an ambitious touring installation project entitled *United Nations*. The project began in 1993 and won't be complete until it visits every country in the world. The installations vary, but they always incorporate huge quantities of human hair gathered from barbershops the world over. The art materially unites all races, all genders, all ages, and all nationalities that comprise the human species. The hair is woven into monumental banners emblazoned with an unreadable script. All the world's populations, speaking all languages, representing all degrees of sophistication, therefore approach the banners as equals. No one can read them, but everyone can be inspired by their utopian vision of global unity. The work literally weaves kinship among all peoples.

1. The divergent tactics chosen by Sacks, Pogacnik, and Gu were all designed to bolster the positive aspects of globalism and/or diminish its negative affects. Select one example of a global threat and create a work of art in which you apply the approach that you believe will most improve the situation.

2. Globalism is apparent in world music, world cups, world wars, world politics, world premieres, world travelers, and the World Wide Web. It is less apparent in paper clips, shoelaces, peanut butter, and combs. Select an item that you own that consists of one kind of substance. Track the stations it has visited backwards, from where it was sold to where it was stored, to where it was packaged, to where it was processed and mined or harvested as raw material. Create a work of art documenting the journey of this item from your possession back to its source. Does it embody global exchange?

3. Establishing local currencies, community gardens, neighborhood recycling facilities, and material exchanges are some ways to reassert the advantages of localism. Create an art work that engages, exclusively, indigenous materials and conditions. Create another art work using manufactured items that are imported.

    A. Compare the emotional and spiritual aspects of creating these art works.

    B. Compare the environmental impacts of these art works. Which used more energy or caused more pollution?

    C. Present your art work to several people you know. Compare your experience of personal display to the impersonal display of art in museums, and/or to published accounts of your work.

    D. Would the conclusions derived from these comparisons also apply to walking to work versus commuting? Would they apply to staying home during vacations as opposed to traveling?

(1) The Gaia hypothesis was conceived by the British scientist James Lovelock in 1979.
(2) Lawrence Fremont. http://www.exchange-values.org
(3) Andre Rigobert. http://www.exchange-values.org
(4) Shelley Sacks, A Banana Is Not An Easy Thing, 2002 http://www.exchange-values.org
(5) Ian Cook, et al. Commodities: The DNA of Capitalism http://www.exchange-values.org
(6) Sacks
(7) Ibid.
(8) Correspondence with the artist, August 8, 2005.
(9) Banana Link. http://www.exchange-values.org
(10) Sacks
(11) http://www.brookes.ac.uk/schools/apm/social_sculpture, April, 2005.
(12) Sacks
(13) Lithopuncture Circles: A manifesto. Proposed by Marko Pogacnik, Sabine Lichtenfels, and Peter Frank. Sempas, Tamera, Weilheim, January 2, 2004.

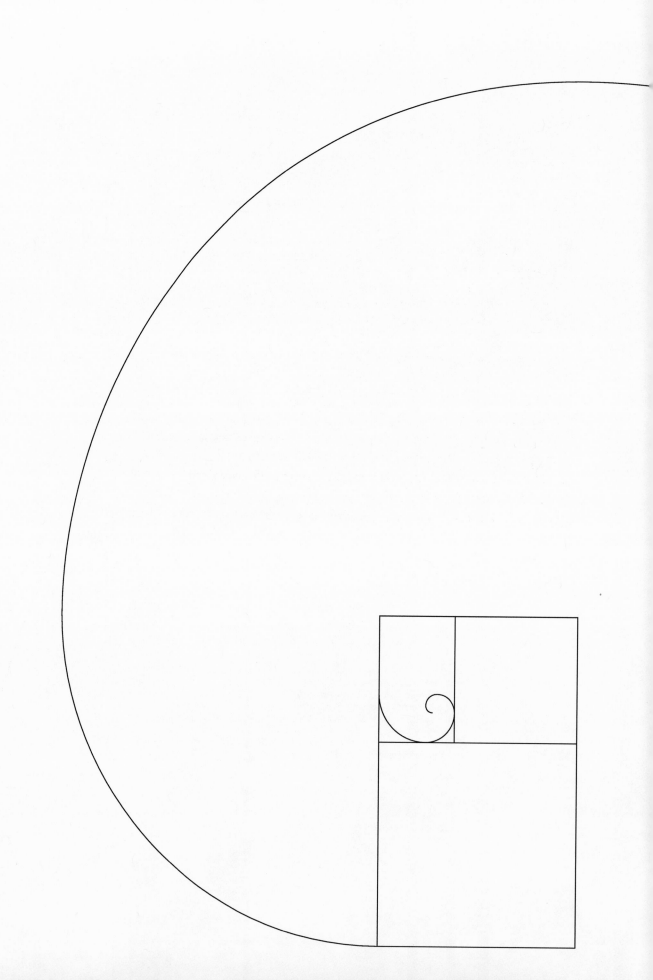

Diversity

Excessive simplicity can result in boredom. Human brains have been known to defend against this state by conjuring hallucinations. Like brains, functional ecosystems thrive on diversity. Biodiversity entails many species interacting in multiple, coinciding networks of positive and negative response loops. The term is also used to refer to the variety of species that exist on the Earth or within an ecosystem. This number has been in continual flux since the origin of life on Earth. Nonetheless, there is widespread concern that current decline in the number of species is both precipitous and preventable

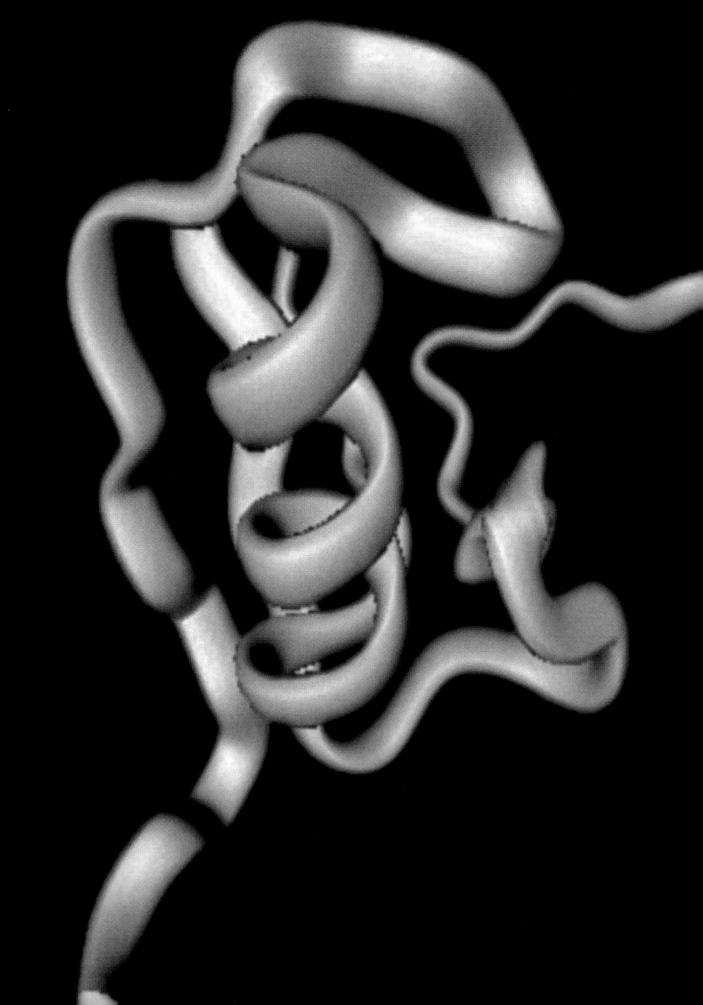

Diversity: An Ecocentric Interpretation

Because diversified systems seem more productive, stable, and resistant to perturbations than simpler systems, environmentalists anticipate that the cumulative loss of species will decrease the ability of ecosystems to tolerate changing environmental conditions. As habitats cease to provide requirements to sustain life, various populations dwindle, while others are obliterated. Some causes of extinction, such as meteor crashes, cannot be averted by humans. But humans are implicated in recent reductions of such richly diversified plant and animal habitats as rain forests, coral reefs, and floodplains. Current technologies for draining, plowing, logging, paving, mining, constructing, and so forth are altering ecosystems on an unprecedented scale. Mono-agriculture, for example, removes and replaces diverse species of native herbs and grasses by committing acres to the cultivation of a single, undeviating crop. Furthermore, mono-agricultural practices often exterminate populations of insects, mice, birds, deer, and wolves to keep the cultivated crops from feeding any species other than humans.

It is estimated that species loss now stands at 27,000[1] species per year. This number seems startling when it is compared to fossil records that reveal total losses, from large vertebrates to insects, bacteria, and fungi, of between 10 and 100 species per year.[2] Some organisms adapt to the conditions resulting from human activities. Other species perish. It remains to be seen if Homo sapiens itself will thrive in the conditions it has created, like city pigeons, zebra mussels, rats, and kudzu trees, or become extinct, like silver trout, passenger pigeons, Atlantic grey whales, and Great Plains wolves.

Although biodiversity represents a core area of ecological research, the total number of living species in the world remains a mystery. The United Nations Environment Program's Global Biodiversity Assessment estimates the number of known species at 1.75 million, but it also estimates that an additional 5 million to 50 million species have not yet been named. Nonetheless, the following observation is widely accepted: each time the gene pool shrinks, the roster of essential services that organic matter contributes to an ecosystem also shrinks. Living matter captures and stores energy, produces organic material, decomposes organic waste, recycles water and nutrients, controls erosion and pests, fixes atmospheric gases, and helps regulate climate. Each instance of loss strips ecosystems of their defenses against drought, flood, disease, and blight. Since living systems are needed to sustain living systems, the unraveling is self-generating and self-perpetuating. If mass murder of humans by humans is called "genocide," perhaps mass murder of other species should be called "gene-ocide."

As noted above, quantitative accountings of the number of species are not registered exclusively as withdrawals. Deposits of new species occur too. Like extinctions, augmentations in diversity can occur in the absence of human activities, as when organisms mutate after exposure to sunshine, nuclear radiation, or viruses that introduce foreign DNA into the cell.

(Figure 0043)

Species formed in this manner usually evolve so gradually that they are difficult to detect. But increases in diversity can also occur as a result of human practices. We humans began protecting and augmenting biodiversity long before Yellowstone National Park, the Endangered Species Act, the Convention on International Trade in Endangered Species, and the U.S. National Park System were established. In fact, we began manipulating the biological makeup of life forms at the dawn of agriculture, when plant and animal breeding began. Early actions revealed a desire to augment and control differentiation. Contemporary actions reveal impatience with the slow pace of genetic shifts caused by natural selection. Then as now, humans seemed reluctant to rely on fate and statistical odds, and even divine intervention, to provide organisms beneficial to us. We design life forms to serve our interests.

Recently, time-honored transformative techniques have been augmented by new super evolutionary powers that actually design new forms of living organisms at the cellular level. Genetic engineering, cloning, stem cell transplants, and the genetic screening of fetuses allow technicians to tinker with the fundamental materials of life. By controlling DNA and RNA, scientists create new life forms in their laboratories. Eduardo Kac is one of many artists joining this effort. He comments, "With at least one endangered species becoming extinct every day, I suggest that artists can contribute to increasing global biodiversity."[3] When Kac took his own advice by contriving genome sequencing, he introduced this controversial arena into his art practice, attracting both awe and criticism. Some critics interpret his deeds as meddling with the biological fulcrum of life; they prefer to relegate the fate of the Earth's populations to the slow and unpredictable forces of natural evolution. Kac proposes a different scenario. He suggests that by creating new life forms, humans might offset the extinctions caused by their mismanagement of ecosystems.

(Figure 0044)

Eduardo Kac

Born 1962 Rio de Janeiro
1985 Pontifícia Universidade Católica, Rio de Janeiro, BA
1990 The School of The Art Institute of Chicago, MFA

Eduardo Kac's transgenic artwork *GFP Bunny* (2000) consists of the creation of Alba, a live albino rabbit that glows bright green when it is illuminated with blue light. Kac created Alba with a synthetic mutation of the original green fluorescent gene found naturally in the jellyfish *Aequorea victoria*. Kac defends the absurdity of this work by reminding viewers that humans initiated the process of directing rabbit evolution in the 6th century, when French monks began domesticating and breeding them. Human-induced selective breeding, coupled with worldwide migration and trade, produced the morphological diversity that now comprises over 100 known breeds of rabbit. Kac insists that his work is not a breeding project. He explains that the green fluorescent protein that created *GFP Bunny* proves it is a transgenic art project that "reveals the fluidity of the concept of species in an ever-increasingly transgenic social context."[4]

Kac may be exploring the imaginative ruminations of science fictions that are being realized in science laboratories, but he begins at the ultimate beginning–the origin of life. When he chose *Genesis* (1998-1999)[5] as the title for his installation, he was referring both to God as the supreme Creator, and to his own powers to enact the ultimate creative act. He accomplishes this by introducing a new form of life through gene manipulations and transgene modifications. By including references to a sanctified act of creation, Kac evoked a hallowed context for the high-tech transgenic explorations that he defines in the following statement, "Transgenic art, I propose, is a new art form based on the use of genetic-engineering techniques to transfer synthetic genes to an organism or to transfer natural genetic material from one species to another to create living beings. Molecular genetics allows the artist to engineer plant and animal genomes and create new life forms."[6]

The murmuring sound of a distant pulsation establishes the otherworldly aura that greets visitors who enter the hushed gallery where *Genesis* is installed.[7] The dimly lit space is infused with the glow from a large orb that resembles the vastness of the cosmos. But the source of the projection reveals this impression to be false. Instead of God's domain of creation, the circular image originates from a microvideo camera trained on a petri dish. What viewers behold is a magnified view of bacteria replicating in real time, not the eternal grandeur of the firmament. This is Kac's domain of creation.

Kac employed two forms of genetic manipulation to create the bacteria. He inserted a gene from a jellyfish in some. In others he introduced a gene of his own creation . His genesis was neither hallowed nor mysterious. It involved cloning the bacteria he created. Kac utilizes known techniques for moving genes between different species. Such transplants are possible because all genes operate according to universal chemical coding. This means that bacteria, plants, and humans are composed of interchangeable segments of DNA.

In this work Kac applies the concept of translation from genes belonging to different species of life to meanings belonging to different species of language. The genesis of the art work originated with the Genesis story in the Bible. Significantly, it sanctions the manipulations of life by humans: "Let man have dominion over the fish of the sea, and over the fowl of the air, and over every living thing that moves upon the earth."[8] Kac translated this passage, written with the 24 letters of the English alphabet, into Morse code, which he then translated into a code of his devising. This code was then translated into the DNA code that includes four elements (adenine, guanine, cytosine, and thymine). In this manner Kac established a sequence of translations that linked language constructed by humans to a chemical language inherent to life.

Images of the new genetic creations were also translated into digital data and dispatched across the globe. They served as high-tech prophets, scribes, and priests announcing news of a new creation via the Internet. But this was not a one-way communiqué. Kac invited human interaction from Web surfers worldwide and people using the computer console in the gallery. They illuminated the petri dish population by clicking their mouses. The act was rewarded with an astonishing sight. The two kinds of bacteria Kac created glowed. One type was genetically altered by the inclusion of the art gene that carried the coded biblical passage; these bacteria also had a gene that produced greenish-blue fluorescence. The other bacteria did not contain the art gene; they were given a gene for yellow fluorescence. Under ultraviolet light, the invented life forms were radiant. This digital illuminated manuscript shared the aesthetics of its era – it was technologically enhanced and synthesized.

Kac's bacteria thrived in the petri dish, where they manifested that diversifying life forms is now an art skill. The bacteria divided and multiplied and divided again. Observing this amazing phenomenon, however, bore an unexpected consequence. The ultraviolet lights that enabled viewers to observe these newly created bacteria also had the effect of accelerating their mutations by triggering the illumination. Observers joined the artist and became co-creators in a new genesis. The mutations were not only biological. As the UV light caused the DNA to mutate, the letters in the scriptural text that determined the DNA sequence mutated too. The English translation of the first mutation of the bacteria read: "Let aan have dominion over the fish of the sea and over the fowl of the air and over every living thing that ioves ua eon the earth."

Scrambling words attributed to God asserts that science is tampering with unequivocal and eternal truths. Even the Bible is subject to unexplored evolutionary trajectories. Linking cells and words demonstrate that both genetic and electronic alphabets are fragile forms of data whose information is transferable and interchangeable. Kac even applied this principle to his own dominion over the bacteria he had created, by abandoning control to anonymous participants the world over. This communal act of mutation and diversification was later carved into black granite tablets in a work Kac entitled *Encryption Stones* (2001). The stones' jagged contours made them appear as if an almighty force had wrenched them from a mountainside (like Mount Sinai) and that the message imprinted upon them was momentous (like the Ten Commandments). This parody of a commanding power confronts audiences with "the dubious notion of (divinely sanctioned) humanity's supremacy over nature."⁹

Kac's art projects suggest that acceptance of genetic manipulation may require a fundamental shift in value systems. Instead of glorifying the rarity of diamonds or the purity of racehorses, cultures would prize the diversity and the multiplicity of life forms. Kac explains, "The mystery and beauty of life is as great as ever when we realize our close biological kinship with other species and when we understand that from a limited set of genetic bases, life has evolved on Earth with organisms as diverse as bacteria, plants, insects, fish, reptiles, birds, and mammals."¹⁰

(Figure 0045)

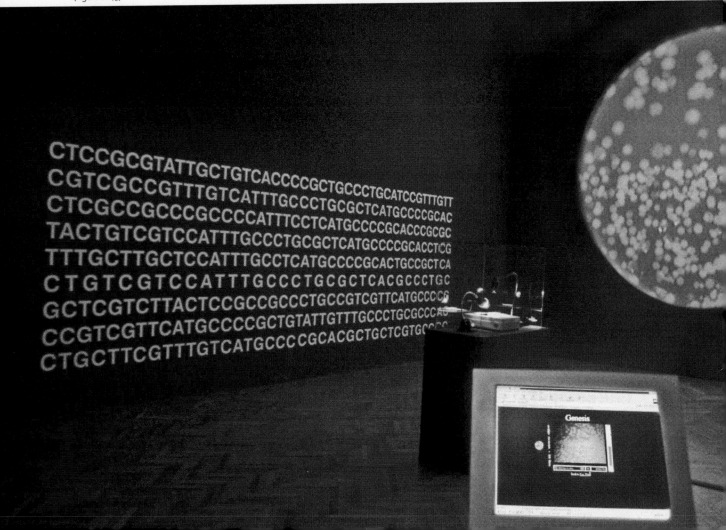

Exploring Diversity

In most college curriculums, scientific studies and cultural studies belong to different disciplines. Likewise, genetic inheritance and environmental influences are approached as separate aspects of the human condition. When they are viewed in conjunction, they typically appear in debates regarding their relative significance in determining behavior. Does nature or nurture rule behavior?

As an artist, Kac enjoys the privilege of crossing professional boundaries by applying genetic engineering to both the biological and cultural considerations of diversity. Natalie Jeremijenko (1966–)shares this approach. The title of one well-known work, *One Tree(s)* (1998), demonstrates that designations of singular and plural are confounded when advanced technologies are applied to diversity. To create this work, Jeremijenko cloned a single black walnut tree one thousand times. She then planted the trees in different public sites around San Francisco. It may seem paradoxical that a project in which one thousand genetically identical trees is included in a discussion of diversity. One Tree(s) earned a place in this context because, as the trees grew, they were not perfect replicas of each other. In fact, they were remarkably distinctive. Each was shaped by its unique microclimate. The seemingly infinite variation of branching patterns, foliage, and growth rates of trees created from a single common ancestor proved that environment plays a significant role in generating biological diversity.

1. There are two sides to most stories, including tales of global warming. If the following report in the *Guardian Unlimited* is credible, species as different as microorganisms and humans will soon confront two alternatives: either adapt or die.

   "Rising global temperatures over the next century could trigger a catastrophe to rival the worst mass extinction in the history of the planet, leading British scientists warned today. Researchers at Bristol University say their studies show that six degrees of global warming was enough to wipe out up to 95 per cent of the species which were alive on earth at the end of the Permian period, 250 million years ago. Up to six degrees of warming is now predicted for the next hundred years by United Nations scientists from the Intergovernmental Panel on Climate Change (IPCC), if nothing is done about emissions of greenhouse gases, principally carbon dioxide, the chief cause of global arming...Conditions in what geologists have termed this 'post-apocalyptic greenhouse' were so severe that only one large land animal species was left alive and it took a hundred million years for species diversity to return to former levels."[11]

   Imagine that the human race has 100 years to prepare for "the second post-apocalyptic greenhouse" and that you have been asked to propose a strategy that would contribute to humanity's chances for survival. Create a work of art on this theme by adapting one of the following approaches:

   A. Improve survival by augmenting the diversity of living conditions. For example, increase the range of temperature to exceed comfort.

B.   Create diversity by manipulating gene structures. For example, design organisms with lungs capable of filtering toxins from the air or decrease the size of organisms to reduce demands for scarce resources.

C.   Improve survival by altering the environment to reduce jeopardy. For example, reduce greenhouse emissions.

D.   Create diversity by inducing mutations within the human race. For example, expose people to controlled radiation.

2.   Genetic breeding and genetic engineering are two of many ways that humans have intentionally augmented diversity. We also increase diversity by constructing parks, botanical gardens, zoos, and gardens. Although in most instances this is a by-product, not the conscious intention of the designers, Patricia Johanson (1940–) designs parks specifically to diversify habitat.

When Johanson describes her design for *Ulsan Dragon Park* (1996), she uses the word "biocultural". The "cultural" aspect of this 912-acre swath of land, situated in the middle of Ulsan, South Korea's leading industrial city, includes a park, a city museum, exhibition complexes, promenade, and Imax theater, as well as sculptural references to Korea's mythological traditions. The "bio" part applies to restored ecosystems consisting of a marsh, pond, creek, floodplain, meadow, wetland, and upland forest. Johanson explains, "*Ulsan Dragon Park* is not just reflecting the cultural history of the past, but also protecting and transmitting genetic information to the future."[12] It accomplishes this mission by creating multiple microhabitats that offer an array of conditions and resources. Her master plan includes ecological landscaping, designing sculptural landmarks, and developing educational programming. Each area functions like a specialty shop offering specific spaces, temperatures, moisture levels, nourishment, and degrees of privacy. For example, the legs of the powerful mythical animal that guards the entrance to the promenade are interwoven with vegetation and nesting shelves for birds. Water flows from the mountainside, over a series of terraces, and down to the floodplain. Here it supports wetland plantings, vernal pools, and a variety of amphibian breeding grounds. A forest playground offers treetop views of forest stratification and canopy habitats. Perhaps the most powerful symbol in the park is the dragon, the mythic mediator between heaven and earth responsible for rain and agriculture. Johanson refers to this cultural tradition but applies it to a biological function by using the dragon as the design for the passage of energy between water, air, and earth. She explains, "The educational program at Ulsan Park is centered around such issues as the survival of species, biodiversity, and the sustainable use of water, forests, energy, and agricultural land."[13] She summarizes her mission by stating, "Perhaps by reintegrating nature and culture within public landscapes, we can ensure the transmission of both ancestral truths and the preservation of the gene pool that ceaselessly provides new forms, meanings and products."[14]

Originally, the term "park" referred to an area maintained as open space where residences, industry, and farming were prohibited. Not even gardening occurred there. These areas functioned as hunting preserves for nobility. Gradually other humans intruded upon these open spaces. This process commenced with gardening. It culminates with the construction of industrial parks, amusement parks, baseball parks, and commercial parks. Patricia Johanson's park provides an example of another type of park. Every one of these models affects the diversity of local plant and animal life.

A. Compare the hands-off policies of a pristine hunting preserve with the hands-on approach Johanson used to construct *Ulsan Dragon Park*. Which policy do you think maximizes diversity? Why?

B. Design the entryway to an industrial park, amusement park, baseball park, or commercial park that provides habitats for diverse species of plants and animals while acknowledging the intended function of the park.

C. What is the relationship between the noun "park" and the verb "park"?

3. Fritz Haeg (1969–) eradicates lawns expressly to diversify plantings in suburbia. The following statement by Haeg summarizes his reasons for believing that his radical actions are warranted: "The mono-culture of one plant species covering our neighborhoods from coast to coast celebrates puritanical homogeneity and mindless conformity."[15] Lawns devour resources while they pollute. Thus, they not only reduce diversity by eradicating every species except cultivated grasses, they accomplish this simplification of the ecosystem by dousing plants with pesticides that are then washed into water supplies with sprinklers and hoses. Haeg extends this logic to the simplification of human experience, "The lawn divides and isolates us. It is the buffer of antisocial no-man's-land that we wrap ourselves with, reinforcing the suburban alienation of our sprawling communities."[16]

Haeg digs up lawns and literally "implants" an alternative model of production. He explains his strategy for demonstrating that this symbol of the American Dream is also a symbol of a suburban calamity by stating, *"We are currently seeking the skilled, eager, and adventurous occupants of one conventional American house on a typical street of endless sprawling lawns. These L.A. citizens should be brave enough to break this toxic uniformity by having their entire front lawn removed and replaced by an edible landscape. As role models they will then proudly devote themselves to the indefinite cultivation of fruits, vegetables, grains and herbs for all neighbors and car traffic to see. This once-hostile front yard will become the southwest regional prototype for the 'Edible Estates' series. We will work in collaboration to create the layout, design and plant specifications. All costs associated with establishing the garden for the first season will be covered."[17]

Lawns are emblems of status. Fritz Haeg highlights the fact that great expenditures of care bestowed upon something that is highly valued can have the effect of decreasing diversity. Your task is to reverse this thesis by creating a work of art about a cultural taboo that either increases or decreases diversity. Taboos represent unwritten social rules that constrain human behavior. For example, there is a taboo in India against eating cattle.

4. Transferring members of a species from one locale to another will decrease diversity if the newcomers out-compete indigenous life forms, and increase diversity if they coexist with indigenous life forms. Create an art work that documents a change in diversity due to the introduction of a foreign plant or animal.

5. The benefits of diversity apply to resources as well as genetics. For example, dependency on a narrow range of resources jeopardizes a species' ability to adapt to environmental change. Compare bison, which derive their primary fuel source from one kind of grass, to people, who depend upon petroleum as their primary fuel source, to create a work of art that enhances human survivability by promoting the use of an uncommon source of fuel.

6. There are five related words in the English language that summarize progressive explanations of beginnings. Some derive from religion. Others refer to science. They are genesis, generate, gene, genetics, and transgenic. Create a work of art that manifests your manner of relating these varying explanations for the origin of life.

(1) "The Current Mass Extinction," Evolution Library http://www.pbs.org/wgbh/evolution/library/03/2/l_032_04.html
(2) Ibid.
(3) Blake Eskin, "Building the Bioluminescent Bunny," ARTnews, Vol. 100, no. 11 (December 2001): 118–119.
(4) Eduardo Kac, GFP Bunny. Artist's statement. http://www.ekac.org/gfpbunny.html#gfpbunnyanchor
(5) Genesis was shown for the first time at Ars Electronica festival in Linz, Austria, in 1999.
(6) Eskin.
(7) Original Genesis music by composer Peter Gena.
(8) Genesis 1:28.
(9) Eduardo Kac, Genesis, in Ars Electronica 99– – Life Science, ed. Gerfried Stocker and Christine Schopf, 310 (New York: Springer, 1999).
(10) Eduardo Kac, GFP Bunny, in Eduardo Kac: Telepresence, Biotelematics, and Transgenic Art, ed. Peter T. Dobrila. and Aleksandra Kostic, 111 (Maribor, Slovenia: Kibla, 2000)..
(11) "Global Warming Could Trigger Mass Extinction," Guardian Unlimited, June 19, 2003. http://www.guardian.co.uk/climatechange/story/0,12374,980561,00.html
(12) Patricia Johanson, "Preserving Biocultural Diversity in Public Parks," NAPtexts(s): A Literary Journal, 2, no. 2 (1997). http://www.patriciajohanson.com/naptexts
(13) Johanson.
(14) Ibid.
(15) Fritz Haeg, "How To Eat Your Lawn." Inhabitat: Future Forward Design for the World You Inhabit, (December 12, 2005). http://www.inhabitat.com/entry_859.php
(16) Ibid.
(17) Fritz Haeg. Artist's website: http://www.fritzhaeg.com/garden/initiatives/edibleestates/main.html

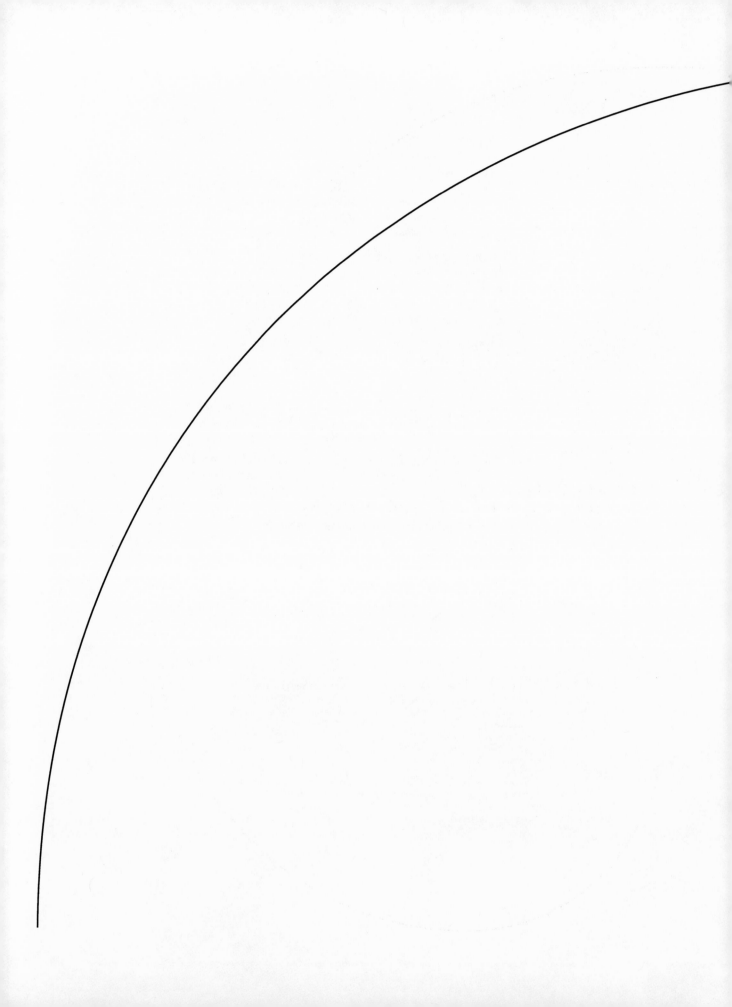

Mercy

The Marvin Gaye song, "Mercy Mercy Me (The Ecology)" rose to the heights of the Motown charts in 1971, and remains to this day a musical legend. In the song Gaye mourns poisons in the wind, oil wasted on the oceans, fish full of mercury, and radiation in the ground. He laments, "What about this overcrowded land? How much more abuse from man can you stand?" The song departs from Motown's usual fixation on broken hearts; it attends to damaged environments in need of mercy.

Mercy: An Ecocentric Interpretation

Mercy is compassionate treatment; an act of kindness designed to alleviate distress. Mercy is a matter of sentiment. It is typically contrasted with justice, the impartial administration of law that assigns rewards or punishments. Justice is a matter of mind. Mercy and justice signify contrasting traits of divine beings. In early history, gods of law contrasted with gods of love. Then these qualities merged into the one God of Christianity, Judaism, and Islam. An all-encompassing God implies the presence of justice as well as mercy. It also makes manifest the superhuman responsibility of determining how these opposing responses should be allocated in real world situations. Humans are still trying to figure out when justice should prevail, and where mercy should be granted.

Mercy motivates people to care for the needy. It is usually praised as an honorable trait, an example of righteous behavior, and a sign of noble intention. Snags, however, arise when the impartial eye of justice is trained upon well-meaning acts of mercy that are directed to ecological considerations. Those who study population dynamics often conclude that mercy may actually interfere with the resilience, adaptability, and vitality of organisms. This is because, in the absence of merciful aid and protection, only fit organisms survive to reproduce. Each generation, therefore, inherits the vigorous traits of its strongest ancestors.

Less-fit organisms lose in the competition for limited resources. Often they are the first to become prey to well-adapted predators. These are unfortunate losses from the perspective of the feeble creatures and merciful observers who tend to sympathize with vulnerable organisms instead of cheering the good fortune of fit organisms. Impartial ecologists, however, are likely to interpret such deaths as a way for the prey's survivors to benefit. Wolves and caribou provide an example of this confusing scenario. Imagine a pack of wolves chasing a herd of caribou. If the weakest caribou falls and gets devoured by hungry wolves, the wolves benefit by gaining nourishment, but the caribou herd benefits as well because the next generation of caribou will not be compromised by its weaker genes. In addition, hearty members will not have to share scarce resources with this weak member. As a result, they become stronger. Merciless competition in the wild maintains the vitality of populations.

In any ecosystem, all organisms are created with equal opportunity to engage in the struggle for their own survival. They can't all be winners. What should be done about the losers?

Should emotion or thought set policies regarding endangered populations of animals and plants?

Should emotion or thought determine how to treat damaged ecosystems?

Should emotion or thought decide how to attend to the less-fit members of the human community?

Even people who make an unqualified commitment to the principle of mercy confront dilemmas:

Should mercy protect loggers with children to feed or old growth forests?

Should mercy be offered to struggling farmers who need water to irrigate or struggling Native Americans who need water to fish?

Should deer starving from overpopulation be offered food drops or should they be hunted?

When an entity has committed an offense and rightful action is being sought, mercy is contrasted with justice. In this instance mercy takes the form of forgiveness and justice takes the form of punishment. However, when an innocent entity is afflicted with stress or weakness, mercy is contrasted with trust, not justice. In these circumstances mercy takes the form of charity; trust takes the form of self-help.

Ecosystems don't conduct misdemeanors so they don't warrant justice and punishment. However, ecosystems can, and often do, experience stress and weakness. In this instance, trust takes the form of faith in the healing capacity of ecosystems to endure adversity and heal their afflictions. Seeking right action becomes a choice between mercy (nurturing) and trust (withholding assistance). Jean Grant teases the concept of mercy beyond its strict dictionary meaning. In her art projects, she questions intense human interventions that produce dependencies, even those that are motivated by compassion.

(Figure 0046)

(Figure 0047)

Jean Grant

Guildford (West Surrey), National Diploma in Design
University of Middlesex, Art Teachers Certificate
University of Westminster, Public Art the New Agenda
University of Liverpool, Post Graduate Diploma interactive media

No green thumbs are required for the gardens referred to in *Gardens of Desire* (1999), a public art project conducted by Jean Grant. Nor is there need for gloves, hedge trimmers, trowels, or other indicators of humans and plants enjoying a mutually beneficial relationship. This work replaces such respectful nurturing with contrasting extremes of interaction. One interaction displays the dependency of plants upon humans that prevails in contrived hydroponics cultivation. The other presents the disengagement of humans from plants that grow in untended thickets.

Hydroponics is a high-tech method for growing plants. There are no weeds to pull and no soil to till. Seed sowing and plant growing are transferred from the variability of soil to the controlled composition of soil nutrients, from fluctuating temperatures of weather to the steady state of architectural interiors, and from the vagaries of rain to the predictable regimens of pipes and pumps. Without constant infusions of care, the plants would not survive. Hydroponics installations resemble intensive care wards in hospitals more than conventional gardens. The plants are dependent upon human acts of mercy.

Thickets, on the other hand, are dense areas filled with close-growing shrubs, small trees, vines, thorns, and weeds. They are so congested, human access is limited, although birds and small animals are present in abundance. In thickets, plants sprout, blossom, and seed in the absence of human interventions. Its flora doesn't depend for its survival upon human acts of mercy. People trust that the vegetation will thrive. Jean Grant amplified the conflict between mercy and trust by adopting contrasting forms of garden ministration in *Gardens of Desire*. Intense cultivation through hydroponics was matched with the absence of cultivation by scattering wild seeds outdoors and then abandoning them to their own resources.

Grant intensified her exploration of the effects of dispensing and withholding care by using wild seeds for both parts of the project. The seeds had been collected by a wild flower center in an effort to preserve plant diversity in the region in Liverpool, England, where the garden was located. Grant then added a human element to this experiment by inviting a group of "wild" young women who were at risk and on probation to work with her to research, plant, and tend the hydroponics gardens, and to scatter seeds and observe the thicket plants outdoors.

The contrasting strategies of mercy and trust regarding the plants held relevance to humans as well. The girls were members of the Venus Young Women's Organization, which provided assistance to disadvantaged girls growing up in a region that was demoralized by multigenerational unemployment, social unrest, and few prospects for improvement. Grant explained that they were surviving like weeds: "This project used wild flowers as a metaphor for the wild young women of the project. It was about the difficulty of growing wild things in institutions. In Liverpool, the population has declined drastically, much like industrial towns in America. The poor remain in depressed cities because they have no other options. These citizens become the experts in city survival. Yet the expertise of poor people is denied them because they are looked down upon as underachieving and uneducated. They don't fit the social criteria. Still they survive. Botanical survival is very similar."[1]

Grant worked with the young women to construct an indoor environment to grow the wild flowers that would normally sprout in the early springtime in that region: cowslip, musk mallow, yellow rattle, ribwort, plantain, white campion, lesser knapweed, ox-eyed daisy, meadow buttercup, red campion, wild carrot, field poppy, cornflower, crested dogstail, and slender creeping red fescue. The girls planted half the seeds indoors under the controlled circumstances of hydroponics. This polythene structure was improvised out of gym bars, 2-by-2 timber, and polythene sheeting. They scattered the other half of the seeds outdoors and were instructed not to intervene in their development. This meant stifling the impulse to nurture the outdoor plants exposed to harsh conditions. In this manner they activated contrasting strategies of mercy and trust.

Because the indoor garden was completely contrived, the girls could determine the plants' growing conditions. Should they lavish the wild flowers with unaccustomed comforts like light and warmth? Should they recreate the harsh conditions of English weather in early spring, when temperatures are cold and there is little sunshine? The girls decided to duplicate the seeds' normal habitat by emulating foul weather indoors. They learned a constructive life lesson when their efforts were foiled by the inflexible regimens imposed by the administration of the school where the garden was constructed. Grant comments, "I thought it would be difficult to grow the seeds inside because we needed to create winter conditions indoors, the climate in which British plants flourish and need at that time of year. But I hadn't expected so many institutional difficulties." First the plants got too much light because the lights could not be turned off during the school session. Then they got too little light because the lights could not be turned on during a holiday recess. Keeping temperatures low was impossible because of central heating. Furthermore, the school was completely shut over the Easter holiday, so the girls could not gain access to care for their plants. In all these ways hydroponics management was thwarted by academic regulation.

Noble efforts and good intentions could not surmount these institutionally imposed misfortunes. The environment designed specifically to exclude the elements produced fragile and straggly plants. The young women described them as "anorexic." At the same time, the seemingly adverse conditions imposed by the English climate suited the seeds planted outside. These plants not only coped, they sprouted and grew into hardy bright green plants. The girls noted this difference and decided to remove the feeble plants from their institutional confinement and expose them to the inclement conditions that were so hospitable for the plants in the control group. The thriving thicket plants were transferred too. Grant

(Figure 0048)

explains the results: "Of course, the move was more difficult for the plants that were brought up in a situation that didn't accustom them to being outside. We tried. The wild ones outdoors transplanted with no problem at all. Very few of the ones reared inside survived."

The girls were impressed by the withered appearance of the plants that had been subjected to institutional regimens and the resilience of the plants exposed to the elements. The contrast demonstrated the disadvantages of being subjected to conditions that are imposed and enforced, even when those actions are motivated by goodwill. Like the plants, the girls too were being provided for within rigid institutional structures. They began to realize that their support system taught them how to conform to rules like showing up on time, but not how to gain their independence. They concluded that regulated institutional care was not going to alleviate child abuse, drug addiction, poverty, and unemployment. This led to discussions about how they might raise their children to provide them with more promising life prospects. Grant comments, "The young women shared ideas about love and care. They saw the plants die even though they loved them as much as they could. They began to understand how the wrong kind of care can make things die. They asked me many questions. Have we loved the hydroponics plants too much? What does it mean to grow up like a wild flower?" Grant concludes, "Young people need support, but they need a different kind of support than they were getting."

The girls who participated in her project were growing up in large, impersonal housing projects that were designed without the involvement of the residents. The girls noted the similarities between their living conditions and their hydroponics garden. The comparison made them aware of the crippling effects of steady-state indoor conditions that abolish evidence of the passage of time and suppress fluctuations in temperature and moisture. They described their living conditions as "unnatural," as unnatural as seeds removed from soil, sun, rain, breeze, pollinating insects, and decaying matter. Grant concurs, "We don't want to accept the industrial model anymore. These institutional situations reduce resilience. They deny the sensuous needs for growing. They deprive plants of the sensations they need. It is also demoralizing for humans to be placed in such controlled settings."

Grant traveled to Cuba in search of a model of care that was not based on mercy and did not result in dependency. She studied the country's unusual urban agricultural practices and learned that Cuban citizens weren't being given aid. Its national history generated policies that promoted trust. "Cubans were starving as result of the fall of communism. They couldn't get weed killers and chemicals and special seeds used in industrial agriculture, so there was a massive turn to organic agriculture. Farmers were given land in trusteeship which they could keep as long as the land was kept fertile and productive. That was 10 years ago. In 10 years they have turned the agriculture of the country around and also the diet of the people. Now Cubans grow 60 percent of their food within walking distance of where it is consumed. This food is grown organically. The government-controlled media instructs people about how to cook vegetables and how to preserve them."

Grant detects signs of positive change in Liverpool. These changes are not, however, evidence of enlightened social service policies. They are the result of a shrinking population. Public housing is gradually being abandoned and vacant factories are being demolished. This trend allows populations to cluster again in the sites of old medieval villages that offered good water and natural shelter and opportunities for agriculture. Grant believes that people thrive when they are sustained by the habitats in which they live. Ironically, it may be economic depression that signals the end of "merciful" ethical policies that impose hothouse conditions and perpetuate a cycle of dependency.

Gardens of Desire planted the seeds of hope for a group of disadvantaged teenagers. Grant emerged more hopeful too. She concludes, "The seed may not come back within an imaginable time, but it can come back in unexpected ways. We are dealing with an unknown, as with the poor. The time that it takes for things to change is very, very long. It can be generational. It hardly ever happens quickly, but it does happen." This art work could serve as a morality tale entitled "Trust in Trust."

(Figure 0046)   Jean Grant, Gardens of Desire, ground preparation and canal clearing, 1999,
                 Courtesy the artist
(Figure 0047)   Jean Grant, Gardens of Desire, summer detail, 1999, Courtesy the artist
(Figure 0048)   Jean Grant, Gardens of Desire, hydroponics seedlings transplanted outdoors, 1999,
                 Courtesy the artist
Full Color images and supplemental images at www.Avant-Guardians.com

Exploring Mercy

1. Painful predicaments accompany the human responsibility of choosing whether weak and dependent forms of life are best served through trust or mercy. Often these decisions are resolved according to subjective loyalties instead of pragmatic judgments. Apply the consequences of trust as compared to mercy to a seriously injured squirrel or some other organism.

    A. Identify whether the organism is more likely to thrive if it is offered mercy or trust.

    B. Identify whether the organism's species is more likely to thrive if it is offered mercy or trust.

    C. Identify whether humanity is more likely to thrive if the organism is offered mercy or trust.

    D. Identify whether the eco system is more likely to thrive if the organism is offered mercy or trust.

    E. What action might you take the next time you encounter a seriously injured animal?

2. Ironically, those who support the principles of mercy because they dislike unbridled competition often get trapped by competing loyalties. Consider the following story:

    "To save the fox, humans are preparing to interfere with nature as a way of undoing the effects of their past interference."[2] This sentence refers to the fox, as well as the bald eagles, that came to Santa Cruz Island in California millenniums ago. The bald eagles ate mostly fish. The foxes ate mostly rodents. Everyone more or less got along, until humans altered the food chain. Domesticated pigs were introduced, and sometime in the 1850s, they began to breed in the wild. Bald eagles, lured by the abundance of piglets, took up residence on the island's jagged cliffs. They also developed a taste for island fox, reducing the fox population to less than one hundred. This leaves conservancy groups with a dilemma: Should federally protected bald eagles be killed to preserve the newly endangered fox?

3. The following news story is amusing, but it is also disturbing, since it suggests that Homo sapiens may become incapable of providing for its own needs.

    "At the London Zoo, visitors can talk to the animals–and now some of them talk back. Caged and barely clothed in a rocky enclosure, eight British men and women were on display beginning Friday behind a sign reading "Warning: Humans in the Natural Environment." The inhabitants of the Human Zoo exhibition sunned themselves on a rock ledge, wearing fig leaves – pinned to bathing suits. Some played with hula hoops, some waved. A sign informed visitors about the species' diet, habitat, worldwide distribution and the threats to its survival." [3]

    Imagine you are the researcher at the zoo studying the current behaviors of a species in North America called Homo sapiens. Your institution is devoted to removing it from the endangered species list.

A.   Write labels describing the average diet and the typical dwelling of the species Homo sapiens currently surviving in the "wild" in urban and/or suburban habitats.

B.   What changes in diet or shelter would you introduce to ensure the long-term survival of the species?

C.   Choose one example of this species' dependency upon a limited resource, such as a type of fuel. How would you deal with this situation to improve its chances of survival? Would your strategy utilize trust or mercy?

4.   In 1970 Robert Smithson sketched an idea for an art work that took the form of a floating island. *Floating Island to Travel Around Manhattan Island* was first realized in 2005, more than three decades after the death of this renowned earthworks artist. Built on a 30-by-90-foot barge and pulled by a tugboat, the fabricated landscape resembled the rocks, trees, and pathways of Central Park.

A.   We know that the specific subject of this work is a planted barge. We cannot know if Smithson intended it to convey a broader theme, such as the relationship between "civilization" and "nature". Assuming it reflects this broader theme, select one of the following possible interpretations of the work, or introduce another. Apply your opinions about trust and mercy.

a. *Floating Island* enacts a heroic rescue mission for nature.

b. *Floating Island* liberates 2,700 square feet of tended nature from the oppressive constraints provided by municipal park services.

c. *Floating Island* is a symbol of nature's precarious dependency upon humans.

d. *Floating Island* embodies the futility of human interventions because it goes round and round and never arrives anywhere.

e. *Floating Island* induces aesthetic contemplation of nature.

f. Other

B.   The following quote by Smithson describes his visit to Great Notch Quarry, located near the tidal estuary that separates New Jersey from Manhattan Island. It may disclose his thinking on the day he sketched *Floating Island to Travel Around Manhattan Island*. Interpret it according to the insight you gain from this quote or any other of Smithson's writings.

"Fragmentation, corrosion, decomposition, disintegration, rock creep debris, slides, mud flow, avalanche were everywhere in evidence. The gray sky seemed to swallow up the heaps around us. Fractures and faults spilled forth sediment, crushed conglomerates, eroded debris and sandstone. It was an arid region, bleached and dry. An infinity of surfaces spread in every direction. A chaos of cracks surrounded us."[4]

5.   Artists who advocate trust instead of mercy might expect to be subjected to public indignation for violating humane principles of compassion. Create an art work that supports an unpopular ecological policy. Structure your work in anticipation of public disapproval. Choose a strategy that either maximizes this response to draw people's attention to the issue, or minimizes disapproval to encourage thoughtful contemplation.

(1)   All quotes from interview with the artist, August 30, 2005.
(2)   Felicity Barringer, "Where There's No Room for All Three of Them," The New York Times (March 5, 2004): A12.
(3)   "At London Zoo, Homo Sapiens Is Just Another Primate Species," By THE ASSOCIATED PRESS, Published: August 28, 2005
(4)   Robert Smithson, The Writings of Robert Smithson, Nancy Holt, ed. (New York: New York University Press, 1979).

Death

Death is the irreversible cessation of all vital functions. The heart stops beating. The lungs stop inflating. The brain stops processing data. Although this syndrome is universal, attitudes about death are variable. In some cultures, death signals a passage into an unearthly realm of existence. In many others, death is viewed as a terminus. The last breath is where biographies end. Within some cultural contexts, it is normal for individuals to approach their own deaths with dread, remarkable to accept their mortality, and madness to cause their own demise. Survivors face a void where a relative, friend, or pet once lived. They grieve. They mourn.

(Figure 0049)

Death: An Ecocentric Interpretation

Death is blameless if old age or accident is its cause. Growing old and dying isn't anyone's fault. Killing is a different story. Killing involves perpetrators and victims, whether it is accomplished by withdrawing a source of sustenance or committing an act of violence. Killings that apply to traitors, murderers, and tyrants are sanctioned by the state. The term "execution" indicates that these deaths involve court judgments and lawful penalties. Yet another killing blueprint applies to military combatants. Wartime deaths are often honored with monuments that commemorate fallen heroes. Others exalt the annihilation of enemies. Deaths of heroes are known as casualties. Deaths of enemies are commonly referred to as fatalities.

Murders can be motivated by passion, or directed by instinct, or planned with forethought. The theme of killing may or may not be associated with guilt. Excusable killings involve individuals who kill in self-defense, governments that kill in the name of justice, and organisms that kill to eat. Finally, distinctive death protocols are applied to plants called weeds and animals known as pests. Wholesale massacres of bothersome organisms are conducted without shame, regret, or recrimination.

In all these ways, death is complicated by civilization. But when it is stripped of culturally laden baggage, it emerges as an incontrovertible law: death means that the molecules an organism borrowed to fill its niche are returned to replenish an ecosystem. From this vantage point, death is exempt from sorrow and rejoicing, ceremony and ethics, religion and law.

Catherine Chalmers forges unlikely intersections between human and animal behaviors that pit victim against perpetrator. Her probing satire exposes the inconsistencies that commonly prevail in attitudes surrounding death.

(Figure 0050)

Catherine Chalmers

Born 1957 San Mateo, California
1979 Stanford University, BS engineering
1984 Royal College of Art, London, MFA painting

First, Catherine Chalmers confronts motives that drive people to kill. Then she applies these motives to the strategies we conjure to carry out these deeds. However, no humans appear in her works. Chalmers utilizes nonhuman surrogates to expose human paradoxes regarding death. She works with bugs, worms, caterpillars, frogs, and other lowly creatures on the food chain. For example, her color C-print series entitled *Food Chain* (1994–1996) presents blatant evidence of murder committed solely for the sake of survival. It differs from the slaughters that abound in news headlines and comprise innumerable narratives designed to entertain us. The media evidently believes that killings prescribed by biology and conducted to satisfy hunger are not newsworthy. In fact, most food producers, packagers, and merchandisers actively suppress the human relationship between killing and eating. Chalmers is equally determined to expose it. She opens her shutter wide and directs her camera at the drive for biological survival as it is being conducted.

Food Chain is a graphic documentation of predators consuming prey. Often, the same creature plays both roles. A frog, for instance, gobbles a praying mantis, which gnaws a caterpillar, which devours a tomato with the ferocity of a hyena. Hornworms, tarantulas, snakes, and mice also enact links within their food chains in front of the lens of her camera. Humans may be absent from these scenarios, but Chalmers offers no reason to assume that we are exempt from the imperative to kill in order to live. This concept is discomfiting to those who are squeamish about the human role in interspecies chains of survival and aggression. Chalmers explains, "Killing to eat is one of the basic processes of the natural world. The way humans have come to interact with their food is different from other predators. What has led us to separate ourselves from something so fundamental? This project would not have been relevant 300 years ago."[1]

The merciless persecutions of cockroach infants and adults by professional exterminators and placid homemakers are testimonies to the psycho-socio disgust of roaches. Entire industries thrive by supplying roach haters with brutal annihilation strategies. The arsenal includes lethal gas, poison, sterilizers, zappers, and traps. Chalmers confronts this reality by feigning it. She selected the American cockroach to represent a common form of calculated, guilt-free murder that generated *Executions* (2003). To create this series, Chalmers staged cockroach executions and then photographed the mock events in gruesome detail. She explains, "I'm doing what we all do with roaches: I'm executing them. But I'm not executing them with a can of Raid or an exterminator. I'm executing them in the manner in which we execute each other. So I'm doing lynching, electric chair, drowning, burning at the stake." These events make dramatic appearances in videos and large black-and-white gelatin silver print photographs.

(Figure 0051)

The well-documented inventory of murderous devices portrayed in the *Executions* series has been used by human societies to kill people believed to be unrepentant sinners or unequivocal threats. The application of this category of killing raises a crucial question: What crimes have cockroaches committed to warrant death sentences? The answer to this question reveals more about human bias and insecurity than about cockroaches. Chalmers comments, "I can think of few other species that are as thoroughly loathed as the cockroach. Yet, interestingly enough, although they carry this heavy burden of hostility, in terms of behavior, they don't do very much. They don't eat in a dramatic way and they certainly don't have the wild sex life of a praying mantis....The American cockroach doesn't sting, doesn't bite, and doesn't carry dangerous pathogens that flies, mice, and mosquitoes regularly do. It's not like having a venomous snake living in the house. There's nothing about the animal that is life-threatening."

Humans have tamed raging floods and traveled to distant planets, but we have not succeeded in outwitting the roach. The futility of human efforts to eradicate cockroaches should not be surprising. Roaches have survived for over 300 million years and through several mass extinctions. Chalmers exposes the humiliating failure of humans to control the roach: "Our homes are now their natural habitat. They are like our alter egos, the shadow that clandestinely follows in our wake."

Chalmers identifies seven reasons why humans view roaches as mortal enemies:

> They lack the aesthetic qualities that humans favor: roaches are not fuzzy, not colorful, they don't have big eyes, and they don't have fur or feathers.

> They are scavengers; scavengers are repulsive because they eat putrid matter.

> They invade sensitive locations; cockroaches trespass on our homes and offices.

> They are nocturnal; cockroaches come out when we are asleep and vulnerable.

> They outnumber us; we feel overwhelmed.

> They live where we can't get at them; a hidden enemy is terrifying.

> They mutate and adapt to technologies designed to control them; cockroaches outwit us.

These reasons explain why these paltry insects elicit irrational dislike. But they do not explain why cockroaches also elicit irrational loathing. Chalmers suggests it is because roaches violate the unwritten decree that all animals that are not classified as pets are acceptable in films, photographs, books, and vacations, but objectionable within our actual lives. "Our hatred of roaches has, perhaps, grown in proportion to the solidity of the boundaries we have erected between ourselves and the natural world. These animals are one of the few now that can, at will, cross over and challenge those barriers. I think at a fundamental level their trespass upsets our confidence in our ability to successfully control and transform nature to suit our needs and desires."

Chalmers not only portrays this rancor, she manages to undermine it by locating her camera close to the annihilation to capture an unflinching view of each cockroach execution. Imagine staring into the eyes of a cockroach clamped by its wrists and neck to a tiny electric chair as a bolt of electricity flares. Consider the effect of a close-up view of a cockroach writhing as flames seem to consume it. Such proximity tends to propel human sympathies across the animal divide. Viewers commonly report experiencing an unexpected surge of compassion for the cockroach in distress, the opposite of their usual callousness about the deaths of insect invaders. At the same time the work arouses uneasiness about lavishing affection on some animals and blithely massacring others. Death dramatizes the divide between "good" nature and "bad" nature, provoking such questions as:

Why do we breed dogs and grind up cows?

Why are we willing to spend millions to save spotted owls and additional millions to exterminate pigeons?

Despite her efforts to set the record straight, Chalmers is not an insect-rights activist waging a save-the-cockroach campaign. "It has never been my intention … to say we shouldn't hate them or shouldn't kill them. I'm not advocating for either their conservation or destruction. What interests me is that we persist in hating them, even though they don't really do anything. It ends up revealing a lot about us."

These bodies of work also reveal a lot about Chalmers. The predators in the *Food Chain* series actually devour their prey. Chalmers lavishes them with care while they are alive, and then chooses not to intervene in their deaths. These murders are committed for survival. Chalmers uses a different approach to present killings that are motivated by revenge and fear. She goes to great trouble to stage the roach executions without actually killing the insects. If fact, her roach actors are indulged like stars. They are bred and raised with loving care in her New York City studio. Nurseries house infants. Rooms are designed and outfitted especially for mating. Other quarters are provided for eating and recreation. The roaches and an odd assortment of other critters inhabit a magical animal kingdom in the midst of Manhattan. This ecological den of death is filled with the peaceful sounds of water falling, crickets chirping, and frogs croaking.

(Figure 0049)   Catherine Chalmers, Electric Chair, Executions series, 2000, 40 x 40 inches, Gelatin Silver Print, Courtesy the artist,
(Figure 0050)   Catherine Chalmers, Caterpillars Eating a Tomato, Food Chain series, 1994-1996, C-Print, 40 x 60 inches, Courtesy the artist
(Figure 0051)   Catherine Chalmers, Praying Mantis Eating a Caterpillar, Food Chain series, 1994-1996, C-Print, 40 x 60 inches , Courtesy the artist
Full Color images and supplemental images at www.Avant-Guardians.com

Exploring Death

1. Chalmers provides an example of zealous efforts to kill a harmless insect. Can efforts to prevent an animal from dying be equally excessive? Consider the following description of efforts to save Keiko, and create an art work that reflects your feelings about the death of this famous whale. Create a satire if you think it is silly. Create a protest poster if you think it is wasteful. Create an epic if you think it is noble. Create an edict if you think it is a matter of public responsibility. Or imagine some other alternative.

   "When Keiko, the killer whale, star of the movie 'Free Willy,' beached himself earlier this month in western Norway, the story of probably the most expensive animal in human history came to an end. By the time of Keiko's death, seven years of effort and more than $20 million had been spent vainly – and unwisely – trying to return the whale to the wild. Although Paul Irwin, president of the Humane Society of the United States, committed his organization to providing Keiko 'with the chance of freedom,' there was never a shred of evidence to suggest that freedom was an aspiration that Keiko shared with the humans who cared for him. ... In a special tank in Oregon, Keiko received remedial training in how to be a proper killer whale – which means killing things. But he never really took to the role." [2]

2. The following excerpt summarizes contrasting human responses to the deaths of animals.

   "There is a schizoid quality to our relationship with animals, in which sentiment and brutality exist side by side. Half the dogs in America will receive Christmas presents this year, yet few of us pause to consider the miserable life of the pig that becomes the Christmas ham. We tolerate this disconnect because ... except for our pets, real animals, animals living and dying, no longer figure in our everyday lives. Meat comes from the grocery store, where it is cut and packaged to look as little like parts of animals as possible. The disappearance of animals from our lives has opened a space in which there's no reality check, either on the sentiment or the brutality." [3]

   Examine your relationship to dead animals by responding to the following questions. Then create an art work on this theme.

   Do you enjoy carnivorous meals?

   Do you wear leather?

   Have you buried a pet?

   Have you killed an insect or a rodent?

   Do you collect road kill?

   Have you dissected an animal?

   Do you hunt or fish?

   Do you disinfect your toilet?

3. By suspending personal attachments from considerations of mortality, death ceases to loom like a fearsome specter and appears, instead, as a wondrous and essential component of eco system dynamics. This is because the death of any individual assures the health of an ecosystem by providing molecules to recycle into new life forms. Ecologically, individual deaths are not cause for bereavement. On the other hand, species' deaths can be reasons for bereavement and preventive action because they reduce diversity.

   Select a contemporary account of death from a film, book, song, advertisement, or work of art. Analyze it from an ecological perspective.

4. The following artists incorporate live animals in their art practices:

   Carolee Schneemann (1939–) communes with cats as erotic and spiritual partners.

   Marina Abramovic (1946–) conducts shamanic rituals with snakes, suggesting that animals provide access to primal wisdom.

   Xu Bing (1955–) engages with silkworms as his collaborators, equal partners in the creation of his art.

   Sam Easterson (1972–) attaches micro video cameras to the heads of such animals as an aardvark, chicken, wolf, water buffalo, and tarantula to capture views of the world from the animals' vantage points.

   Create or design a work of art that reveals how any one of these artists might respond to the death of his or her animal partner. Would the artist cremate the carcass or eat it, take it to a taxidermist, entomb it, expose it to the elements, feed it to other animals, preserve it in formaldehyde, use the parts, or treat it in some other manner?

5. Ecologically, one organism's death is a phase in the recycling of organic molecules, not an end point. But when all the surviving members of a species, in all of their habitats, cease to contribute to the pulse of life on the planet, they constitute evolutionary and ecological end points. Such deaths are known as extinctions. Each diminishment of diversity depletes life's safe deposit box of adaptive strategies for coping with a fluctuating ecological futures market.

   Rachel Berwick (1962–) uses poetic titles to evoke the irretrievable losses caused by extinctions: *Hovering Close to Zero*, *Two Fold Silence*, *A Vanishing*, and *The Last of Her Kind*. These titles accompany haunting materializations of such extinct species as the Tasmanian tiger and the passenger pigeon. Berwick expanded the theme of loss to incorporate humanity in *may-por-e* (1996), an installation in which two Amazon parrots speak an extinct South American language. Berwick was inspired by Alexander von Humboldt (1769–1859), the renowned explorer and naturalist. Humboldt purports to have found a parrot that was the sole remaining speaker of a lost language when he arrived at a Carib Indian village in the Venezuelan rainforest a few days after the tribesmen had exterminated their neighbors, the Maypure. The only survivors were the Maypure's pet parrots. Berwick worked with von

Humboldt's meticulously detailed journals, a bird behaviorist, two linguists, and a sound engineer to train two parrots, Apekiva and Papetta, to speak the extinct language. It took 13 months of intense training in a room with a sign warning, "Only Maypure spoken here." In the exhibition, the parrots were transferred to an aviary created out of translucent material, where they appeared as projected shadows, a visual reminder of material absence and cultural loss. But they could be heard. The larger and noisier the crowd, the more lustily the birds squawked, "mapa" (honey), "arata" (banana) "yapa" (hello), "nukapi" (hand), and so forth.

Create a work of art that addresses the theme of biological or cultural extinction and invent a way to convey your work of art to people who do not seek art experiences in museums or galleries.

6. Performance artist Linda Montano (1942–) did not wait to die to be reborn. Her rejuvenation was inspired by her father's impending death, which occurred in 2004. In 1998, she says, she heard voices beseeching her to return home to care for her aging father. In 2000 she declared this experience a work of art. This art work is integral to Montano's lifelong commitment to investing life with the devotion and ceremony of art. As her father's primary caregiver, she monitored his physical and metaphysical conditions as they evolved day by day, amassing a great quantity of records detailing his food intake, medications, mental state, and bowel movements. The records chronicle his body's gradual relaxation into death. At the same time, Montano's father manifested a heightening of his creative powers. As he gradually lost the ability to speak, walk, feed, and dress himself, he began to paint. His faltering hand produced images of stirring beauty. They are spare and mysterious, reflective of his transitional state of being. Montano's intimate communion with her dying father is offered to the public in the form of a video. Titled *Conversations with My Father* (2005), the video portrays her multiyear process of assuming the tasks her father could no longer perform. She bathes him, feeds him, dresses him, and ministers to his comfort. Montano attends especially to her father's artistic blossoming. Her synchronous awakening is evident even as she repeats each chore day after day. Dying also stirs a life-enhancing sensation among viewers, who observe that the tedium of hospice care offers an opportunity for growth and enrichment. In this manner, spiritual attunement to death, psychological acceptance of death, and biological processes of death are united.

    Please comment on death's capacity to be physically and/or spiritually replenishing.

(1) All notes based on an interview with the artist, September 2004.
(2) Clive D. L. Wynne, Op/Ed, The New York Times (December 27, 2003).
(3) Michael Pollan, "The Unnatural Idea of Animal Rights," New York Times Magazine (November 10, 2002): 57.

Decay

Uncontestable evidence of the unpopularity of decay is revealed by its popularity among heavy metal music circles. Musicians flaunt their counterculture ideals by exulting in decay, along with depravity, the apocalypse, nuclear annihilation, and environmental devastation. Bands not only savor these grisly themes, they brandish them in the names they select: Lust of Decay, Man Must Die, Mortal Decay, Decomposition, Still Life Decay, Putrid Pile, Decay of Salvation, Garden of Decay, Artery Eruption, and so forth.

(Figure 0052)

(Figure 0053)

Decay: An Ecocentric Interpretation

When death occurs, an organism ceases to consume food, water, and air. But this does not mean it ceases to affect its environment. Once the organism is no longer able to organize its chemistries, the energy bonds and molecules of the corpse dismantle. Death releases the molecules that comprised the organism's physical substance. Through decomposition, the materials are sorted and then liberated to resume processes in which they engaged prior to being temporarily recruited to form a living being. The final act of every organism involves relinquishing its storehouse of essential ingredients to the environment, where it becomes available for utilization by other organisms.

This process is efficient and grizzly. When someone's heart stops pumping blood, tissues and cells are deprived of oxygen and begin to die. Some die within minutes. Others persist up to 24 hours after death. However, the millions of microorganisms in the body's intestines don't die with the person. These organisms break down the dead cells, starting in the intestines and then raiding other parts of the body. At the same time that dead cells are discharging enzymes that cannibalize themselves, decomposing tissues are releasing green lung fluids that trickle out the mouth and nostrils, and tissues are emitting gases that blister the skin and swell the abdomen. After death, there is always a mess. Decaying organic matter isn't pretty and it smells foul. But the ecosystem provides a clean-up crew. Turkey vultures, carrion beetles, and some maggots, fungi, and bacteria are ecological sanitation workers. They savor the mess, feed upon it with relish, and recycle it through their digestive tracts.

Biological decay belongs to the cycling processes of the life force in which nutrients are fed back into the system. Still, few of us welcome decay as an opportunity for renewal. Depending upon circumstances, decay is more likely to be viewed as a sign of weakness, evidence of malfunction, or a precursor to death. Defenses against decay take the form of wood preservatives, food stabilizers, rust retardants, Botox injections, cryogenics, fluoride treatments, and climate-controlled interiors.

The essential qualities of decay become apparent when it is compared to entropy, the tendency for all matter and energy in the universe to evolve toward a state of inert uniformity. Entropy measures how much energy has dispersed from a specific locale. It can be observed when hot pans cool, when water flows downhill, when air blows out of a punctured tire, when cream spreads throughout the coffee. Whereas decay means matter is being dismantled and readied for reconstitution, entropy disperses energy and makes it less useful. Entropy charts change in the direction of less organization and less complexity, while life supports organization and complexity. Decay is integral to life processes.

Damien Hirst might be considered a heavy metal visual artist, since he has no intention of conforming to social niceties or offering aesthetic pleasantries to his audience. He exults over decay, drags his audience into the fray, and confronts them with perishable materials perishing. It seems that the only decomposition he strives to postpone is the decomposition of his own reputation as a blunt conveyer of unwelcome truths.

(Figure 0054)

Damien Hirst

Born 1965 Bristol, England
1986–1989 Goldsmiths College, University of London

Humans are adept at producing copious varieties of prejudices – race, nationality, ethnicity, gender, and sexual orientation are just the beginning. Fat bodies, short statures, big noses, flat feet appear on the list. The aging phases of the life cycle are targets of especially strident bias. This prejudice is so widespread that it has spawned an arsenal of pharmaceutical, dietary, surgical, physical, and spiritual weapons to fight against the encroachments of time. Popular attitudes regarding the deterioration of the flesh cluster around squeamishness, horror, and repulsion. Few share the biologist's acceptance and the ecologist's appreciation of this vital process. Damien Hirst offers the perspective of a daredevil artist, "What the fuck are we doing, dying? It's so delicious, it's so beautiful, it's so fabulous. You don't have to buy a microscope to see how fabulous it is. The real gear, the stuff that we're living in, rots. And things that rot are so fucking colorful."

Hirst used crash-course tactics to purge viewers of their prejudice about decay when he confronted them with the severed head of a cow infested with flies and maggots. The cow that contributed its head to this sculpture is not sacred in this context. What was sacred, however, was the belief system it undermined: art should convey beauty, refinement, and proficiency. Not surprisingly, the sculptural installation provoked fury.

A Thousand Years (1990) was a sensation in the infamous Sensation exhibition that launched the careers of a hot young brood of British artists. The work consists of a steel-framed, glass-sided 7-by-24by-7-foot vitrine that is divided into two compartments. One side refers to the cool formalism of minimalist art; it contains a white cube with a portal opening on each side. The other side demolishes the formalist connection; it holds the rotting remains of the cow head. The eerie blue light that bathes this macabre scene originates from a ultra-violet fly zapper suspended over the head. These compartments are home to swarms of flies and maggots that mate and birth in one cubicle, and feast and die in the other. Viewers encounter glass walls stained in yellow fly excrement, rotting flesh, and shriveled fly corpses heaped beneath the zapper.

Hirst is not a purist in his pursuit of material decay. When the stench became unbearable, he burned the head and carefully emulated its rotting flesh with ketchup, dog food, and other substances the flies would eat. "You've got to take the smell away to make people look at a fucking horrible thing…. I'm not into stinking everyone out of the gallery. I'm into drawing them into the gallery." Whether or not the sensationalism of the art work is a sign of the artist's lunatic lust for publicity, as some critics attest, it addresses society's lunatic denial that matter decomposes. Facial creases and moldy bread are objects of disgust.

A Thousand Years utilizes a method for instilling tolerance that resembles sensitivity trainings, or T-groups as they were called in the 1960s. As part of the human potential movement, the training was designed to help people

(Figure 0055)

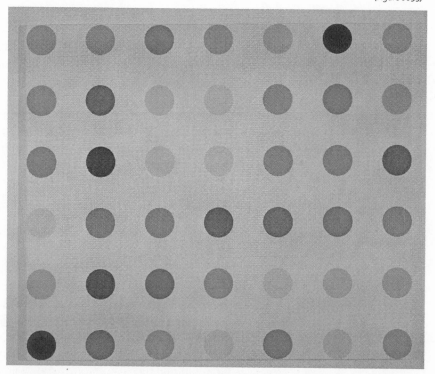

overcome prejudices in interpersonal relationships. Instead of relying on intellectual arguments or other mechanisms of mind control, sensitivity training takes a confrontational approach: "Fan the resentments of the people of a community; fan the latent hostilities of many of the people to the point of overt expression – search out controversy and issues ... An organizer must stir up dissatisfaction and discontentment."[3] Hirst applies this strategy to art. He even expands it, since the prejudice against decay is not only social, it is also personal and environmental.

Hostilities inherent to the theme of this work were fanned by the sight of unsightly messes. Hostility came especially from mea–eaters, who learned that they share a taste for slaughtered cows with maggots. It was intensified by animal rights advocates whose sympathy for animals did not affect their disgust for flies and maggots. Ultimately, Hirst proves the impossibility of facing death as an abstract concept. Each fatality is a reminder of our personal mortalities. We share this mortality with 5 billion people who are now alive on earth, and who will decay with us within the next 100 years.

Pharmacy retains the theme of decay, but reverses the blunt approach used in *A Thousand Years*. In this series of installations and paintings, Hirst addresses a nationwide obsession with pill popping by populations seduced by the power of drugs. The Pharmacy paintings consist of rows of equally spaced, multicolored dots on a pure white background. The colors are decorative, but they also function thematically. Each dot is a color chosen by a drug manufacturer for pills and lozenges: Apomorphine, Adenosine, Anthroylouabain, Pardaxin, etc. No two hues in a given painting are identical, indicating the tremendous quantity of available drug choices. Likewise, the lack of patterns among the colors indicates the randomness of our pill-swallowing habits. Instead of confronting viewers with unsettling realities, the spot paintings bolster delusions about our ability to thwart decay. These cheerful paintings not only "whitewash" signs of decomposition, they "paint over" our fears. As Hirst puts it, "We all die, so this kind of big, happy, smiling, minimal, colorful, confident facade that medicine and drug companies put up is not flawless—your body lets you down, but people want to believe in some kind of immortality."[4]

The *Pharmacy* installations expand on the obsession with prescription drugs to retard age, prevent disease, and relieve discomfort. Apothecary bottles, vials, and boxes are aesthetically arranged in medicine cabinets and on shelves. In some installations, Hirst adds surgical instruments and anatomical models that reflect medical efforts to halt mortality. But mortality makes an appearance as well. In one installation of *Pharmacy*, Hirst cut holes in the gallery windows to allow flies to enter the space to enjoy honey and get zapped by the insect-o-cuter he installed. In addition, the installations include thousands of individually handcrafted pills. They appear indistinguishable from the originals. Hirst explains that the pills were fashioned synthetically because "real pills decay. They rot. They're made to dissolve in your body."[5] They were remade so that the *Pharmacy* series could offer viewers a surrogate fulfillment of their unattainable desire for permanence. Hirst describes the series as "an unfailing formula for brightening up peoples' fucking lives."[6]

A third body of work goes beyond dreaming of preventing decay. It actually accomplishes this goal. The results, however, are not triumphant. Instead, they announce another distressing truth: death alone is not sufficient to halt the aging process. To last forever, one must be both dead and pickled. In order to make this point, Hirst submerged a menagerie of fish and mammals, whole and sliced, into embalming baths of formaldehyde. He presents the specimens as sculptures. *The Physical Impossibility of Death in the Mind of Someone Living* is the revealing title of a preserved and disinfected tiger shark. The title seems autobiographical. Hirst confesses, "I am aware of mental contradictions in everything, like: I am going to die and I want to live forever. I can't escape the fact and I can't let go of the desire."[7]

Hirst is banking on art to fulfill his desire. The title *A Thousand Years* signals his determination to outlive his body by establishing a reputation that will survive one thousand years. "Art's got the aura because people are prepared to hold it close to them for thousands of years, longer than people. Whereas you chuck videos in the bin, you smoke fags, and you throw your clothes away, and you buy Charlie, and your food rots in your fridge, and you redesign your house. But art, they spend ages repairing it."[8]

But even a professional life span of one thousand years does not satisfy Hirst. A billion years may be required before his work can be fully appreciated. "Diamonds have been around for billions of years…. It's carbon with the shit taken out of it. And things become clear after billions of years….

They don't become clear, they become sparklingly fucking clear."[9]
And yet, in the final analysis, even that astronomical figure cannot halt
disintegration. "Eventually this whole world will wear out to nothing.
And that is caused by entropy. It's a force…. It's the action of the world
on itself. Put it up, it's going to eventually come down."[10]

Hirst confronts the flesh and guts that belong to normal existence. He dares us to
join him in this pursuit. This requires relinquishing our futile hopes of
surmounting transience, and facing the inevitability of decay. For many,
this task demands nothing less than surrendering old attitudes and
learning to think all over again—ecocentrically.

(Figure 0052)	Damien Hirst, A Thousand Years, 1990, Glass, steel, MDF board, cows head, fly zapper, bowls of sugar water, 84 x 168 x 84 inches, Copyright, the artist, Courtesy Jay Jopling/White Cube, London
(Figure 0053)	Damien Hirst, A Thousand Years, detail, 1990, Glass, steel, MDF board, cows head, fly zapper, bowls of sugar water, 84 x 168 x 84 inches, Copyright, the artist, Courtesy Jay Jopling/White Cube, London
(Figure 0054)	Damien Hirst, Pardaxin, 2004, Household gloss on canvas, 44 x 52 inches, Copyright the artist, Courtesy Jay Jopling/White Cube (London)
(Figure 0055)	Damien Hirst, Pharmacy, 1992, Installation: Cabinets, glass, desk, apothecary bottles, medicine bottles, chair, fly zapper, foot stools, bowls and honey, 9feet 5 inches x 22feet 7 inches x 28feet 3 inches, Copyright the artist, Courtesy Jay Jopling/White Cube (London)

Full Color images and supplemental images at www.Avant-Guardians.com

Exploring Decay

1. "Hirst's Shark Disintegrating"[11] is the headline of an article reporting that Damien Hirst's renowned sculpture of the shark floating in a tank of formaldehyde is disintegrating and will need extensive conservation to prevent it from further deterioration. The sculpture was purchased by an American billionaire hedge fund manager named Steve Cohen for $12 million. Conservation scientists and natural history specialists note that the shark has deteriorated noticeably to the naked eye since it was first unveiled at the prestigious Saatchi Gallery in 1992. The formaldehyde solution in which it is suspended is murky, while the skin of the animal is showing signs of wear and tear.

    A. Do you think Damien Hirst would delight in this news? Explain your answer.

    B. The renowned art historian and philosopher, Arthur C. Danto, has written extensively about the death of art. Danto applied death to the conceptual and stylistic components of art making. Hirst's shark introduces physicality into this discussion by raising two issues:

        a. The intended preservation of the art object.

        b. The unintended decay of the art object.

    How do these issues apply to Danto's theories?

2. The following statement applies the theme of decay to therapeutic treatment:

    Maggots savor rot. Some doctors are beginning to enlist these miniature flesh-eating ghouls as surgeons in the hygienic field of biotherapy. They are revising a practice that was used in the American Civil War, whereby maggots are placed on wounds of soldiers to facilitate healing. The larvae savor dead or infected tissue, leaving healthy tissue alone. Furthermore, as they munch, they secrete chemicals that stimulate the production of healthy tissue. If people can overcome their squeamishness, maggots may some day help us avoid the problems associated with antibiotic-resistant bacteria.[12]

    A. If you were wounded, would you choose to heal yourself by murdering bacteria or feeding maggots?

    B. Would pro maggot therapy or anti-bacteria therapy be more likely to be supported by the federal Environmental Protection Agency or Food and Drug Administration?

    C. Explain.

3. Taxidermy is the art of removing the guts of dead animals, stuffing the skins with matter that does not degrade, and mounting the specimens to achieve a lifelike appearance. Distinctly different components of taxidermy appear in the work of the sculptor Gillian Jagger (1930–) and the art group Gelitin, whose members include Ali Janka (1971–), Florian Reither (1967–), Tobias Urban (1967–), and Wolfgang Gantner (1988–). They demonstrate contrasting approaches to the theme of decay in art.[13]

A. Gillian Jagger is known for floor-to-ceiling sculptures created out of decayed matter. In addition to using weathered board, rusted tools, rotted tree trunks, and animal bones, she has been known to include a mummified cat. All these visceral materials confirm the progression from vitality to vulnerability to death to decay. A work entitled *Matrice* (1997) introduced an even more graphic representation of this theme. It included the actual corpse of a deer that Jagger found as roadkill. To emphasize its deadness, Jagger wrapped a chain around its neck and suspended it. Then she secured the deer in resin to prevent further decay. In this manner, she adapted the theme of decay to a conventional artistic context. The front of the animal was mostly skeletal with ragged bits of flesh, while the back was intact. By enhancing the entrails of the deer with paint, Jagger imbued decay with aesthetic richness. The work defied cultural norms by transforming squeamishness into an uplifting connection to a primal life process.

Jagger uses a real dead animal, halts its decay, and flaunts the animal's death. Create a work of art that addresses the theme of decay in the manner of Gillian Jagger.

B. Gelitin created a huge, 200-foot-long stuffed rabbit that now lies on top of a mountain in the Swiss Alps. The rabbit's belly adds 20 feet to the height of the mountain. It lies on the ground, face to the sky, arms spread wide, legs flopping on the downward slope, entrails spilling from its body cavity. Gelitin convinced the citizens in the nearest town to allow Hase (Rabbit) to remain undisturbed from 2005 until the year 2025. This allows time for the overscaled rabbit corpse to disintegrate into a formless mess. The artists guarantee this theatrical spectacle of decay because they fabricated the rabbit out of straw and wool, two very unstable materials. The decaying process began even before the last stitch of the sculpture was knotted. Gelitin member Tobias Urban explained, "The rabbit is feeding a lot of other kinds of life. There are already mushrooms and grass growing out of it. And there is lots of this yellow thing appearing. It looks like the doll vomited. I saw birds nesting. Cows want to lie down on the straw. The straw is radiating warmth as it decays. This is appealing to animals in winter. It is creating niches that protect animals from the wind. It stores moisture between the legs. It makes all these animals feel like home."[14]

Gelitin uses a fake dead animal and encourages its visceral deterioration to dramatize the process of decay. Create a work of art that addresses the theme of decay in the manner of Gelitin.

4. Are the following questions absurd or reasonable? Decide by answering them from an ecocentric perspective, not from human sentiment.

   A. Are people who choose cremation or cryogenics selfishly withdrawing their bodies from the food chain?

   B. Should tax money fund research to extend human life?

   C. Breast implants, artificial joints, pacemakers, and prostheses do not degrade biologically after death. Should this fact affect preparation of corpses for burial?

   D. Should environmental agencies inspect corpses for drugs, growth hormones, preservatives, pesticides, asbestos, and other toxins before permits are granted for burial?

   E. Should free burials be provided to those willing to be buried in depleted soils?

5. Design and/or perform a graveside ritual, eulogy, sacrament, or obituary that presents death as a gift to the ecosystem.

---

(1) Damien Hirst and Gordon Burn, On the Way to Work (New York: Faber and Faber, 2002), 79.

(2) Ibid., 181.

(3) Saul D. Alinsky, Rules for Radicals: A Pragmatic Primer for Realistic Radical,s (New York: Vintage Books, 1971).

(4) "Turner Prize History: Damien Hirst," Tate Online, http://www.tate.org.uk/britain/turnerprize/history/hirst.htm

(5) Hirst and Burn, 116.

(6) Ibid, 119.

(7) Tate Online.

(8) Hirst and Burn, 167.

(9) Ibid, 164.

(10) Ibid, 182.

(11) Gareth Harris. "$12,000,000 Spent on Rotting Shark," Art Newspaper (May 2, 2005). http://www.shark-trust.org//cgi/main.asp?newsfirst=591

(12) See http://www.ucihs.uci.edu/com/pathology/sherman/home_pg.htm and usm04.discoverlife.org/mp/20q?go=http://medent.usyd.edu.au/projects/maggott.htm

(13) See Weintaub, Linda, Cycle-Logical Art: Recycling Matters for Eco-Art. Avant-Guardians: Textlets in Art and Ecology Art (New York: Artnow Publications, 2006).

(14) Interview by author with Tobias Urban, November 30, 2005

Dirt

Organic humus and its living occupants are components of dirt. Humus might qualify as a prop for a horror movie because it consists of a grisly admixture of defecated matter from slimy invertebrates and the decaying corpses of virus, yeast, mold, and bacteria. Some other mucky ingredients of humus include twigs, needles, bark, and leaves of plants; and hairs, nails, bones, and skins of animals, all in various stages of decomposition. Environmentalists focus on the wondrous functions performed by this gruesome substance. Humus provides a home for the microscopic organisms that jump-start the food chain upon which we and all other forms of life depend. By channeling moisture and air through dirt, living organisms mix the strata of the earth's mantle and enable plants to grow.

Dirt: An Ecocentric Interpretation

Dirt, like humus, elicits derogatory connotations. Dirty words are rude. "Dirt cheap" and "dirt poor" signal the lowest of low value. These phrases link the Earth's principal life-sustaining substance with squalor instead of fertility. They reveal a deep-rooted preference for the sanitized products of technology, engineering, and industry. The word "soil" also carries the distasteful connotations of filth, sewage, and refuse, despite the fact that topsoil is where most roots and microorganisms are located. The dirty thoughts related to soil can be traced to the Indo European word for pigsty, "souil".

Yet people who actually grow plants are proud connoisseurs of dirt. For them, its vital role in perpetuating the cycles of life dignifies the substance. Soil specialists also savor its multiplicity. Soil samples from deserts, swamps, coasts, basins, woods, and jungles are as varied as the vegetation they support. Experts have identified eleven separate soil orders and assigned proper names to 14,000 distinct varieties.[1] Another wondrous function of dirt is to provide a home for an immense diversity of life forms. The microbe population in a single teaspoon of topsoil is believed to exceed the entire human population on the planet today.

Dirt also varies in health and sickness. Healthy dirt is productive. Sick dirt cannot sustain plant growth. Although there are many causes of illness in dirt, one major cause can be traced to mono-agricultural farmers who grow the same crop year after year. Depletions of soil nutrients lead to dependence on chemical fertilizers. This practice sets off a chain of events that compromise fertility: populations of microorganisms decline, tiny waterways through the soil diminish, and the production of organic matter that binds soil together shrinks. As a result, soil becomes less

porous, water runs off the surface – requiring farmers to depend upon irrigation – and irrigated land can become too salty to support plant life.

Degrading valuable topsoil is currently a problem. It could become disastrous if United Nations estimates come true. The UN reports that nearly 800 million people are currently undernourished. This grim statistic could increase to 1.5 billion by 2010.[2] Feeding this huge population in 2030 will require increasing food production by 60 percent. The UN estimates that 20 percent of the additional production will come from increases in land used, 10 percent from more harvests per year, and 70 percent from higher yields.[3] Since meeting this unprecedented challenge depends upon soil health, many environmentalists are seeking the means to assure high yields without depleting the productive capacity of soil. Conservation agriculture is being proposed as an alternative to techno-agriculture. In essence, conservation agriculture rotates crops, allows fields to lie fallow, and leaves crop residues in fields after harvest. These methods replenish nutrients while reducing mineralization, erosion, and water loss. But assuring soil health is not simply a job for farmers and gardeners. Dirt is depleted by thoughtless land use, negligent waste disposal, unrestrained logging, and so forth.

How can new outbreaks of soil sickness be prevented? How can ailing soils be cured? Humans can create soil health by attending to its needs as one might attend to a beloved pet. Dirt is living matter. It thrives and multiplies when it is fed and tended. Joe Scanlan has taken the initiative by establishing criteria for world-class dirt and then fulfilling these criteria in his art practice.

(Figure 0056)

Joe Scanlan
Pay Dirt

SEPARATE TO OPEN   RESEALABLE PACKAGE   PRESS TO CLOSE

IKON

EARTH

(Figure 0057)

Joe Scanlan

Born 1961 Stoutsville, Ohio
1984 Columbus College of Art and Design, BFA
1985 The School of the Art Institute of Chicago, MFA

Gold was not the only form of profit that resulted from the American gold rush in the middle of the 19th century. Many of the slang phrases that continue to enliven the English language can be traced to the rustic imaginations of miners prospecting for riches in the Old West. Such verbal gems as chiseler, hold your horses, land's sake, pony up, slower than molasses in January, and the whole kit and caboodle derive from this source. So does the term pay dirt, which Joe Scanlan chose as the title of a work of art that consists of high grade potting soil.

Pay Dirt (2003) required five years to research and develop. Instead of prospecting in fields and stream beds for ready-made soil or studying commercial simulations, Scanlon tested ways to assemble the raw ingredients for soil from common consumer by-products. His investigation culminated when he transformed a gallery into a mini-processing plant that actually produced dirt. The dirt was packaged and sold to visitors as part of the exhibition.

"Pay dirt" is slang for discovering something of value. Miners hit pay dirt when they strike gold, a substance that is prized by humans who relish its glistening beauty. It is also valued because of its ability to withstand the elements. But gold is irrelevant to ecosystems because ecosystems do not benefit from inert substances. Instead, they thrive on festering rot that is highly reactive, even if it is not pretty. Scanlan's title suggests that dirt is worthy of high value when the productivity of a "fertility standard" replaces the beauty of the "gold standard." In other words, dirt pays when its metaphoric association with grime and squalor is exchanged for its function.

Scanlan's productive composting is always conducted locally. Collecting the ingredients from the environs of the gallery where the dirt is being processed and sold demonstrates that all gallery visitors can participate in dirt production. Alternatively, anyone can purchase a bag on the web at http://www.thingsthatfall.com/dirt.php. The price of $20 per bag makes it possible for most people to become art collectors. But they are not collectors in a conventional sense. Because Scanlan's dirt is made of 99.85 percent postconsumer waste, it includes common ingredients like used coffee grounds and other household garbage. Collectors learn to save products they would normally discard. Furthermore, instead of preserving his dirt in a pristine condition, Scanlan encourages collectors to manifest dirt's value as a life-generating medium in their gardens and window sills.

At the same time, presenting his product hot off the assembly line in full view of gallery visitors challenges cultural associations of value with rarity. Scanlan adopts the conventions of commercial enterprise by presenting his mass-produced art work unapologetically as a consumable commodity. He packages his dirt in six-liter, zip lock, polyethylene bags with attractive three-color graphics. This strategy encourages viewers to explore dirt as a source of enlightenment. It invites critics to analyze dirt's life-enhancing attributes. It also helps collectors experience pride in owning high-quality dirt.

Pay Dirt expounds upon this ecological lesson by demonstrating that not all dirt is created equal. There are three basic types of dirt: loam, sand, and clay. Loamy soils are considered best for propagation, but they vary too. The formula for an ideal loam is 45 percent mineral particles, 5 percent decomposing organic material, 25 percent water, and 25 percent air. *Pay Dirt* was conceived, designed, and crafted to manifest dirt excellence. Scanlan aspired to achieve dirt's idealized form as classical artists once idealized the human form. He called his creation *IKON EARTH*, suggesting that his plant-growing medium is worthy of devotion, like an icon. This achievement, however, is not dependent on the assessment of art critics. Evidence of its superiority is provided by the official government certificate that accompanies Patent No. 6,488,732, certifying the fertility standards of Scanlan's sculpture.

According to the advertisement that is also part of Scanlan's art project, IKON EARTH contains nitrogen for robust growth, potassium for water uptake, phosphorus for bountiful fruiting and flowering, calcium for root development, magnesium for photosynthesis, sulfur for promoting new growth, and a high-action exchange rate for maximum absorption of nutrients. The text explains this miracle blend is "released in the slow, organic way plants like best, without the use of synthetic polymers or nutrient-retardants.... IKON EARTH is a work of art and may be harmful to some plants. Like all viable growth media, IKON EARTH contains naturally occurring bacteria that fight pathogens and cycle nutrients to plant roots.... For best results, use your hands."[4]

Scanlan is candid about his motives in striving to create dirt in its ideal form. He admits he wishes to achieve personal acclaim. "My best chance of leveraging any money or power or influence in such a culture as the United States stems directly from my ability to invent and exploit images that no one has ever seen before." Instead of seeking originality through self-expression, his quest for originality takes the form of ecological service. "Artists have very little power. In America, a ruthlessly money-based and moralistic country, persons who make things that are of no obvious or immediate value are viewed as charlatans at best and, at worst, parasites."[5] Scanlan sought to elevate the value accrued to him and his art product by applying his originality to an essential function and using the product "as a kind of soapbox on which to stand and proclaim my proud participation in—but distinction within—the global economy. I'm very proud of this dirt and I enjoy making it. It is a vital, healthy product that promotes nourishment and beauty wherever it goes. So, as both a product and a philosophy, I want *Pay Dirt* to be infectious. I want it to get under people's fingernails."[6]

(Figure 0058)

(Figure 0056) Joe Scanlan, Pay Dirt, installation view, 2003, Coffee grounds, sawdust, gypsum, egg shells, bone meal, blood meal, Epsom salt, Three tons, arrangement variable, Courtesy of the artist and IKON Gallery, Birmingham, England

(Figure 0057) Joe Scanlan, Ikon Earth, Pay Dirt display detail, 2003, Flexible ink on polyethylene, zip lock closure, potting soil, 17 x 14 x 4 inches, Courtesy the artist and Galerie Micheline Szwajcer, Antwerp

(Figure 0058) Joe Scanlan, Cone-shaped display of Ikon Earth and Black Country Rock, 2003, Flexible ink on polyethylene, Pay Dirt potting soil, MDF, paint, 90 x 48 x 48 inches, Courtesy the artist and Galerie Micheline Szwajcer, Antwerp

Full Color images and supplemental images at www.Avant-Guardians.com

Exploring Dirt

1. Imagine that a 4-H Club established a competition and provided ribbons to people who raise excellent breeds of dirt. Create a work of art that presents your submission to the competition. Present your dirt as living matter that is thriving and multiplying because it is well-fed and tended, like a beloved pet.

2. "Wanted: Tons of Fake Moon Dirt: NASA Experts Developing Standards for Simulated Soil."[7] This headline referred to a presidential announcement that robotic missions to the moon were being resumed. NASA immediately began conducting research into technologies and systems that could maximize the use of lunar resources to support human space exploration from the moon to Mars and other destinations. That means living off the moon instead of hauling materials from Earth. In NASA language this goal is referred to as In-Situ Resource Utilization (ISRU). It means using local materials and energy to support human and robotic exploration. Years ago NASA produced tons of lunar simulant from volcanic ash of basaltic composition.

   NASA's dirt was headline news because it offered the allure of otherworldly exoticisms. Scanlan's homeland dirt did not enjoy this media advantage. His dirt was figuratively and literally downtrodden, despite the fact that it is productive while NASA dirt is sterile. Furthermore, his dirt is real while NASA's dirt is synthetic. Do these contrasting public perceptions contradict or confirm Scanlan's regret that, "In America… persons who make things that are of no obvious or immediate value are viewed as charlatans"? Do you think Scanlan jeopardized his own reputation by creating dirt? Has NASA jeopardized its reputation by creating dirt?

3. Like Scanlan, the following three artists elevate the value of essential substances that are largely ignored by the public. They focus on air, water, and pollen.

   Air: Laurie Palmer created a series called *Oxygen Bars* (2005), stainless steel cylinders on wheels that contain miniforests. The forest is a bonsai-sized version of Hays Woods in Pittsburgh, Pennsylvania, an area that currently has unacceptable quantities of airborne soot and other pollutants. Air quality is further threatened by plans to conduct mountaintop removal for coal extraction and to construct a racetrack and gambling casino on the site. Trees naturally filter dirty air through leaf mass and bark textures, and through transpiration and photosynthesis. Palmer's minuscule woods function in this way too. People can snort the oxygen generated by each bar via attached tubing or they can inhale it by lifting the lid. Signage and maps printed on the bars link this air-cleansing operation to the threats to Hays Woods. The text also invites residents to propose alternative uses for the land. In an artist's statement Palmer explains, "The primary goal of the Hays Woods Project is to generate a sense of public ownership in this resource."[8] Air is free. Like most free goods, it also tends to be subjected to neglect and abuse.

Water: Mark McGowan (1967–) is an artist who stirred outrage within the art community, among environmentalists, and throughout the popular media with an infuriating art work called *Running Tap* (2005). It consisted of a simple action: McGowan turned on a cold water tap at the House Gallery in south London with the intention of leaving the tap running for one year. At the end of the year, 15 million liters of water would have run down the drain. McGowan yielded to public pressure after nearly 800,000 liters of water had run down his drain. He decided that *Running Tap* had accomplished its mission by then because it had directed attention to the 1,000,000,000 liters of water that trickle out of London's leaking Victorian water mains each year.

Pollen: The method that Wolfgang Laib (1950–) engages for gathering the material for his art work boggles the mind of anyone who values efficiency and labor-saving strategies. Laib walks through open fields and forests, stopping at one flower blossom at a time. Gently and methodically, he flicks grains of pollen into a jar. Gradually, over the course of an entire growing season, he may gather enough pollen to serve as the material and theme of a single sculpture. By reenacting the symbiotic rapport between bees and the plant kingdom, Laib performs a rite of survival and procreation that is foreign to many contemporary humans. His sculptures often consist of simple pilings of pollen upon the floor. These sparse art works radiate the visual, tactile, and olfactory beauty that is inherent to the pollen itself. Their ceremonial elegance hallows a substance more commonly associated with allergies.

Joe Scanlan, Laurie Palmer, Mark McGowan, and Wolfgang Laib all advocate on behalf of a substance that sustains life but receives little recognition or care. Instead of relying on representations and symbolic expressions, these artists allow the medium to convey their message. Choose a neglected substance that is essential for survival. Use this substance to create a work of art that strives to increase its visibility and improve its care.

4. The very low value assigned to dirt is probably correlated with the common perception that dirt exists in very high quantities. This implies that it can be squandered without consequence. The following statements contradict this impression:

¾ of Earth is water and ¼ of Earth is land

½ of land is available for human use.

¼ of land available for human use is too rocky for food production.

½ of land available for human use is too wet or too dry, too hot or too cold for food production.

¼ of land available for human use is available for food production. This means that only $1/32$ of the earth's surface is available for food production.[9] Create a work of art that attempts to elevate the value people assign to dirt by instructing them about its scarcity.

(1) William Bryant Logan, Dirt, the Ecstatic Skin of the Earth (New York: Riverhead Books, 1995), 180.

(2) Ecohealth, "What's Left to Eat? Food and Water: Enough for Everyone, http://www.ecohealth101.org/whats_left/eat3.html

(3) BBC - Science & Nature – Countryfile(?) - Eco Top Ten - Agriculture http://www.bbc.co.uk/nature/environment/conservationnow/global/agriculture/page3.shtml

(4) Artist's website: http://www.thingsthatfall.com/dirt.php

(5) Joe Scanlan, Commodify Your Dissent: François Piron Interviews Joe Scanlan." http://www.thingsthatfall.com/interviews-piron.php.

(6) Ibid.

(7) Leonard David "Wanted: Tons of fake moon dirt: NASA experts developing standards for simulated soil" http://www.msnbc.msn.com/id/6861900/.

(8) Artist's statement, "Groundworks: Environmental Collaboration in Contemporary Art 3 Rivers 2nd Nature," in the STUDIO for Creative Inquiry at Carnegie Mellon University. 2005 http://3r2n.cfa.cmu.edu/groundworks/Palmer%20Proposal.pdf

(9) "How Much is Dirt Worth?" http://extension.usu.edu/AITC/teachers/pdf/dirt/worth10.pdf

Topics for Discussion

Jean Grant includes hydroponics and academics in an art work about dependency.

Dave Burns and Matias Viegener include hydroponics and academics in an art work about empowerment.

Reverend Billy Talen discourages people from shopping.

Shelley Sacks encourages people to shop.

Catherine Chalmers creates death.

Eduardo Kac creates life.

Damien Hirst presents decay as an aesthetic spectacle.

SUPERFLEX uses decay as a functional energy source.

Joe Scanlan creates a commercial product for use in urban and suburban settings.

SUPERFLEX creates a commercial product for use far from urban and suburban settings.

Rob Fischer introduces organic processes into art galleries and most people are enchanted.

Damien Hirst introduces organic processes into art galleries and most people are horrified.

Reverend Billy Talen delivers dramatic evangelical sermons to confront audiences with the urgency of behavioral reform.

Shelley Sacks evokes sensual experiences to stir awareness of behavioral reforms.

Eduardo Kac incorporates the unintended consequences of unsuspecting participants into his work to yield unpredictable outcomes.

SUPERFLEX requires participants to learn a skill and use it thoughtfully and thereby yield unpredictable outcomes.

Jean Grant uses plants as a metaphor for humans.

Catherine Chalmers uses insects and animals as metaphors for humans.

Joe Scanlan's dirt is suspended in a state of pure potential.

Rob Fischer's dirt is actively productive.

Pioneering Themes for Exploration

We cannot surmise what early humans did for fun or how they expressed their feelings, but we can assume that when archaic peoples surveyed their environments, they focused on weather patterns, water, plants, animal, stones, and sticks. This is because their survival depended upon discriminating edible from poisonous vegetation, and harmless from dangerous animals. Likewise, they would discern materials useful for tools. For the same reason, contemporary city dwellers and suburbanites are likely to note bottled beverages, traffic conditions, and ATM locations. Human cognition automatically culls bits of data that are pertinent and ignores irrelevant inputs. We remember only some past experiences. We address only some present circumstances. We use only some data to predict future events. Our cultural context determines these inclusions and exclusions. It also determines choices of artistic themes.

Like maps, works of art highlight specific categories of information by directing attention to certain features and ignoring others. They differ as much as road maps, topographical maps, celestial maps, and chromosome maps. Little by little, art maps and cultural maps are being redrawn to acknowledge ecological considerations. Consciousness is being diverted away from concern for human health, security, and fulfillment. Instead of attending exclusively to an individual's immediate gratification and eternal rewards, they address responsibilities for the short- and long-term well-being of ecosystems.

Evidence of this cultural shift is apparent among artists whose themes address expenditures of energy, or depletions of resources, or habitat restoration, or the long-term environmental consequences of shortsighted business policies, and so forth. Eco-artists are exploring a vast new domain of thematic opportunities that encompass all habitats, all life forms, and all time scales. To date, settlement in many thematic zones is sparse. Some remain unexplored. Although the full scale of this territory cannot even be estimated until its parameters are charted, three categories of approach are evident. They are identified below, along with examples of the exhilarating topical opportunities they provide.

Proverbs

Shared ecological information.

These themes map published scientific data and popular cultural assumptions. Because they convey shared truths, they resemble proverbs.

All life depends upon sunlight.

Nonhuman life forms tend to acquire only as much energy and materials as they require for survival.

Ecosystems benefit from diversity.

Because everything is used in a functioning ecosystem, there is no waste.

Form optimizes function.

Change is inevitable.

Organisms are interdependent.

The Earth's material resources are limited.

Biological matter inevitably degrades.

All organisms participate in the food chain.

All organisms cause changes in their habitat through their life processes.

Theories

Personal ecological opinions.

These themes map an artist's attitudes, guesses, impressions, judgments, and reactions. Because they can't be proven, these themes resemble theories.

The best way to understand the environment is through:

>scientific study
>
>statistical analysis
>
>divine revelation
>
>observation
>
>functional interactions
>
>other

Organizations of ecosystems resemble:

>chaotic confusions like buckets of worms
>
>geometric structures like beehives
>
>intricate connecting forms like spider webs
>
>angular accumulations like quartz crystals
>
>other

The environment is best understood on the scale of a:

>single cell
>
>organism
>
>watershed
>
>continent
>
>planet
>
>solar system
>
>universe
>
>other

The following entities would benefit if humans left them alone:

>plants
>
>bacteria
>
>climate
>
>shorelines
>
>weather
>
>aquatic life
>
>forests
>
>other

Blueprints

New cultural imperatives.

These themes introduce new manifestations of eco-centrism that override existing egocentric principles. They resemble blueprints outlining future prospects for civilization:

> systems of production and exchange
>
> technologies of production
>
> methods of education
>
> forms of literacy
>
> concepts of design
>
> definitions of wealth
>
> measures of success
>
> concepts of time
>
> forms of celebration
>
> other

The artists whose works are featured in this textlet are participating in a sweeping reevaluation of the status quo. They are formulating the maps that guide personal decisions and public policies. It is not necessary for readers of this book to adopt the themes these artists chose to benefit from their examples, or to agree with their policies. Readers can still share their faith in the map-making powers of art. These powers transcend theme and approach. They are expressed in the following ways:

> Issues artists highlight attract public attention.
>
> Behaviors they conduct establish models of behavior.
>
> Values they assert are discussed.
>
> Solutions they propose are tested.
>
> Functions they perform are adopted.

In conclusion, no work of art can be all-inclusive. All artists select specific time frames, locations, subjects, and perspectives. Some conduct this process intentionally. Others proceed unconsciously. In both cases, works of art function like maps that highlight an artist's values, principles, priorities, fears, and desires. These are the elements that comprise an artist's theme. Ecocentric themes are rarely on the map of existing values. They are more likely to be found off the mark and over the top. They disrupt the status quo. Artists who believe that change is both necessary and beneficial, and wish to participate in the evolution of culture, will find opportunities galore among ecocentric themes. This book concludes with an invitation to venture into a frontier of hope and promise.

Linda Weintraub is the author of Avant-Guardians: Texlets in Art and Ecology (2006–ongoing) and founder of Artnow Publications. She wrote In The Making: Creative Options for Contemporary Artists (2003) and Art on the Edge and Over: Searching for Art's Meaning in Contemporary Society (1995). From 1982 to 1993, Weintraub served as the first director of the Edith C. Blum Art Institute, located on the Bard College campus, where she originated 50 exhibitions and published more than 20 catalogues. She is curator and coauthor of Lo and Behold: Visionary Art in the Post-Modern Era, Process and Product: The Making of Eight Contemporary Masterworks, Landmarks: New Site Proposals by Twenty Pioneers of Environmental Art, Art What Thou Eat: Images of Food in American Art, and The Maximal Implications of the Minimal Line. Since leaving Bard College, Weintraub curated a nationally touring exhibition, IS IT ART? She cocurated the internationally touring exhibition Animal. Anima. Animus with Marketta Sepalla. Prior to her appointment at Bard College, Weintraub was director of the Philip Johnson Art Gallery at Muhlenberg College. She has taught both contemporary art history and studio art. Weintraub served as Henry R. Luce Professor of Emerging Arts at Oberlin College (2000–2003). She holds a Master of Fine Arts degree from Rutgers University. Weintraub is currently a contributor to the international art journal Tema Celeste. She lectures frequently on contemporary art and its intersection with ecology.

Skip Schuckmann is currently working as an ecologically oriented land sculptor in upstate New York and southern California. His art practice is site-specific and involves multiyear engagements with the hardscape, biological materials, and owners of the sites. These engagements have combined his academic training in science and his professional activity as an artist and educator. Schuckmann holds a BA degree in wildlife biology from Colorado State University (1967), and a Master of Arts in Teaching (1972) in experiential education from the University of Massachusetts, Amherst. His formal educational engagements have involved experimental programs at the Golden High School in Golden, Colorado; Woolman Hill School in Deerfield, Massachusetts; Ojai Foundation in Ojai, California; the Randolph School in Wappingers, New York; and Oberlin College in Oberlin, Ohio.

SMCL

3 5151 00215 1280

209316

Made in the USA